HOW TO MA[ ]

WIT[ ]

BREAKOUT
TRADING 2.0

Analyse the Stock Market Through
Candlestick Charts

INDRAZITH SHANTHARAJ

Manjul Publishing House

First published in India by

Manjul Publishing House Pvt. Ltd.
● C-16, Sector 3, Noida, Uttar Pradesh 201301 – India
Website: www.manjulindia.com

Registered Office:
● 2nd Floor, Usha Preet Complex, 42, Malviya Nagar,
Bhopal 462 003 - India

Distribution Centres
Ahmedabad, Bengaluru; Bhopal, Kolkata, Chennai,
Hyderabad, Mumbai, New Delhi, Pune

This edition first published in 2023
Fifth impression 2024

ISBN 978-93-5543-241-4

Printed and bound in India by Thomson Press (India) Ltd.

Disclaimer

This book is sold with the understanding that the author is not engaged in rendering legal, accounting, or any kind of advice while publishing this book. Each individual's risk appetite and expectation from the market are different. All ideas, opinions expressed or implied herein, information, charts, or examples contained in the lessons are for informational and educational purposes only and should not be constructed as a recommendation to invest and trade in the market. The author disclaims any liability, loss, or risk resulting, directly or indirectly, from the use or application of any contents of the book.

Technical analysis is a study of past performance, and past performance does not guarantee future performance. Investors and traders are advised to take the services of a competent expert before making any investment or trading decision.

This book is
Dedicated to the two gurus of my life:

Stock Market and Sadhguru

Contents

Introduction to the Updated Edition   9

Acknowledgments   11

Section 1 – Positional Breakout Trading

1. Breakout Trading Is the Most
   Underrated Trading Technique   15
2. Read This Before You Draw a Trend Line   23
3. How to Identify a Genuine Breakout
   in 60 Seconds   34
4. Execution Matters a Lot in Trading   47
5. Top 10 Questions and Answers on
   Breakout Trading   71

Section 2 - Intraday Trading

1. Read This Before You Jump into
   Intraday Trading   79
2. How to Analyze Market Sentiment
   in 5 Minutes?   87
3. Market Open Always Gives a Clue
   for the Open-Minded Trader   111
4. These Intraday Systems Can Fetch
   You a Lot of Profits   118

Section 3 - Options Trading

1. Why Trade in Options?   141
2. What is an Option?   143
3. Options Trading Jargon   146
4. Long vs. Short in Options Trading   148
5. ITM, ATM, and OTM in Options Trading   150
6. Greeks in Options   152
7. How to Trade Options   154
8. Role of Time Decay in Options Trading   161
9. Importance of Strike Price in Options Trading   163
10. Options Trading – Buying or Selling?   165

Section 4 - Trading for Beginners

1. Why Everyone Should Know About
    Stock Markets   171
2. Some Basic Concepts You Must
    Know About the Stock Market   173
3. Technical Analysis vs. Fundamental Analysis   180
4. Types of Charts in Trading   189
5. Avoid These Stocks to Protect Your Wealth   198
6. Different Types of Trading   202
7. Support and Resistance Matter a Lot in Trading   206
8. Chart Patterns   213
9. Technical Indicators   226
10. How Successful Traders Develop
    a Trading System   243

Introduction to the Updated Edition

The COVID-19 pandemic impacted every single living being on this planet, either directly or indirectly. Before the pandemic, I started teaching breakout trading to a group of people, all with different backgrounds, and once the lockdown was imposed, I began receiving many queries on a daily basis.

Unfortunately, most questions were duplicates of each other. Therefore, I decided to prepare a small PDF document containing clear information about the positional breakout trading system along with a Q&A section. I aimed to save my time by sharing the document with them.

Everyone found the document very helpful, and I was recommended to publish it as a book. I was skeptical about publishing it because a typical book contained a minimum of 200-300 pages, whereas my book's first edition had only 72 pages. I also didn't have contacts at any traditional publishers.

I came across Amazon's Kindle publishing process and decided to publish my book on breakout trading there as it was free, and anyone could publish a book on their platform.

So I asked my friends Mr. Sanket Gajjar ('San' on Twitter) and Mr. Harneet Singh Kharbanda to review my book. After implementing their suggestions for the book, I published it on Kindle.

To my surprise, the book had a fantastic debut, and thousands of people read it just in the first week. At the same time, I started sharing my live breakout trades on Twitter.

This book has been translated into many languages in the last two years. Also, **it was one of the top 3 best-selling books on Amazon India in the self-published category in 2021.**

Most people liked the book, but a few came up with the suggestion to include some of the basics of technical analysis. Some people also asked me to include some information on how to take breakout trades in intraday trading.

So, I have decided to include those topics in this updated version. This book contains four sections:

Section 1 – Positional Breakout Trading

Section 2 – Intraday Breakout Trading

Section 3 – Options Trading

Section 4 – Technical Analysis for Beginners

If you are a beginner who doesn't know about the stock market, please read Section 4 first and then proceed with the remaining content.

Acknowledgments

Many helped me in the preparation of this book. I would like to thank all my trading gurus, as they taught me everything about trading.

I would like to thank TradingView (https://in.tradingview.com/), as all the charts which are used in this book are taken from there.

Two large-hearted traders helped me immensely with the preparation of this book. They are Sanket Gajjar and Harneet Singh. More power to both of you guys, now and always!

Thanks to both Nandini Panchakshari and Team Pothi (https://pothi.com/), who helped with editing and proofreading.

Shrinivas Joshi (https://www.shrinivasjoshi.co.in/) has prepared an attractive cover page for my book. Special thanks to him.

I have a big list of friends who have supported me in all my book ventures. I will be forever grateful to all of them.

Indrazith Shantharaj
July 2022

Section 1

Positional Breakout Trading

1

Breakout Trading Is the Most Underrated Trading Technique

How do you differentiate a genuine breakout from a false breakout?

This question had been bothering me for many years. Back then, I was working in a software firm and I used to attend many workshops on trading during the weekends just to ask this one question. I was pretty sure that if I could just crack this question, it would help me immensely with both positional trading and intraday trading. However, I didn't get any satisfactory answers from most trainers.

On one such weekend, I was attending a two-day workshop on trading conducted by a famous technical trader in India. I thought to myself, "I will surely get the answer to my question this time." He explained many trading-related concepts. However, I was just waiting for a chance to make my inquiry. Even one and a half days later, I didn't get an opportunity to ask my question, as many other participants surrounded him during lunches and coffee breaks.

Time was ticking, and I had just one hour left. From my experience, I knew that trainers left early on Sunday evenings with the excuse of having to catch a flight. He was busy explaining some concept, and assuming I might not get an opportunity to clarify my doubt over a Q&A session (if there even was one), I gathered the courage to interrupt his speech with my question.

I was hoping that he would explain the answer using charts. To my surprise, he switched off the projector and came forward. Then he started telling everyone how his big connections in Mumbai and Wall Street traded. He described how they took large quantities, how they considered auspicious days like a full moon or Diwali, and how they took into account the rise in sea level to add to their quantity. Finally, he concluded that most of the breakout days in any script were closely associated with such auspicious days, or with a good day related to the particular script!

I was frustrated by his answer and angry at myself for wasting two days of my life, and so I decided not to attend any workshop on trading going forward.

With this state of mind, I went to a remote place within the Western Ghats in Karnataka, India. It had an old temple, and I somehow felt positive vibes in the area. The next morning, I woke up early and went for a walk. After the hike, I went inside the temple and meditated there for some time.

When I was coming back to the guest house, I saw a mother chicken roaming with its baby chicks. All the baby chicks were following the mother except for one. Sometimes it was leading the group, sometimes it went far away from the group, and sometimes the mother chicken followed the baby chick along with its other babies.

Unconsciously, I stopped walking and started observing their activity. Within a minute, I had got the answer to my question! I couldn't believe that I finally found the solution to a problem which had been haunting me for several years. Unfortunately, I didn't bring my laptop with me, but I was too impatient to wait there. I checked out from the guest house and drove back to my place. It was a 400 km drive, and I didn't take a single break in between.

Once I reached my home, I immediately began to check my findings using the charts. Fortunately, my idea was correct, and save for this first chapter, the remaining content of the book is a detailed expansion of that single idea!

What is a Breakout?

The Investopedia website says, *"A breakout is a stock price moving outside a defined support or resistance level with increased volume. A breakout trader enters a long position after the stock price breaks above resistance or enters a short position after the stock breaks below support."*

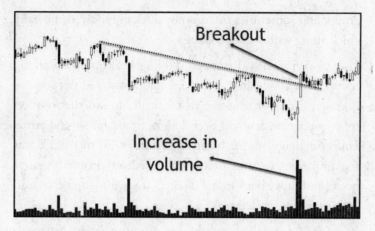

Image 1.1 – An example of a breakout (a break of the resistance trend line)

In Image 1.1, the price broke the resistance trend line with high volumes. Similarly, if the price breaks the support trend line, few recognize it as a breakdown.

To keep it simple, we will focus only on the breakout.

What is a False Breakout?

A false breakout is also recognized as a 'failed break'. Investopedia's definition for a failed break is: *"A failed break occurs when a price moves through an identified level of support or resistance but does not have enough momentum to maintain its direction. Since the validity of the breakout is compromised, and the profit potential significantly decreases, many traders close their positions. A failed break is also commonly referred to as a false breakout."*

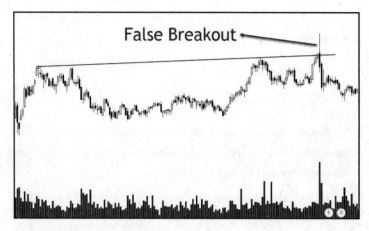

Image 1.2 – An example of a false breakout

In Image 1.2, the price showed the characteristics of a breakout. However, it failed in its attempt and broke on the opposite side.

Why Is This Information Important?

In my opinion, every trader (whether they are intraday, swing, positional, or a scalper) should know how to differentiate between a genuine breakout and a false breakout.

Do you know why?

Because every entry and exit in any trade should come through a breakout or a false breakout opportunity!

(That doesn't mean that other trading techniques will not work. My explanation holds true if a trader is looking for the best entry and exit points.)

Let me explain.

It's important to understand the two herds that exist in the market:

1. **Smart money**

2. **Dumb money**

Smart money refers to institutional investors – big sharks who have money and information power and who give direction and momentum to markets.

Dumb money refers to nonprofessional traders – retail traders who often try to make quick money.

Do you agree that it's always a good idea to follow the smart money?

If yes, check the chart below carefully.

Image 1.3 – The action plan of smart money (daily chart)

If you look at Image 1.3, the smart money has prevented the fall three times with significant buying volumes.

Besides, the price has consolidated for over eight trading days before the breakout. It indicates two things:

1.   Smart money is not willing to sell at this price level.

2.   Dumb money got exhausted with its selling.

If you look at Image 1.4, it's evident that smart money had a clear action plan.

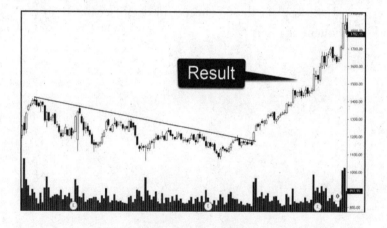

Image 1.4 – The action plan of smart money (daily chart) – result

So, it's always better to take entry when we get the confirmation from smart money (you can't make trades along with them unless you are one among them).

Besides, it's significant to plan an exit if you can judge that smart money is exiting. A trading system should accommodate such entry and exit points, because only entry and exit decide the fate of your trade, irrespective of your reputation, experience, or qualifications!

This breakout trading system consists of three critical components:

1. **Drawing proper trend lines**

2. **Identification of real breakouts**

3. **Trade execution**

I will explain these concepts in detail separately in the subsequent chapters.

2

Read This Before You Draw a Trend Line

Before you draw a trend line on any chart, ensure it's not an operator stock and that price action is smooth. If either don't apply, it's better to avoid it, as there is a high probability of hitting your stop-loss.

Some examples are given below.

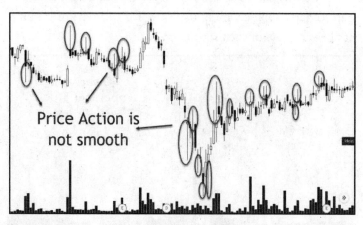

Image 2.1 – Price action is not smooth (Example 1)

If you look at Image 2.1, it has a lot of selling wicks and buying wicks, which are not suitable for this type of trading. It can trigger your buy order or stop- loss order and can move in the opposite direction. It's better to avoid such scripts.

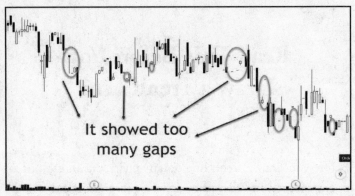

Image 2.2 – Price action is not smooth (Example 2)

Another example is shown in Image 2.2. It has too many gap scenarios, which are not suitable for this type of trading. It's better to avoid such scripts.

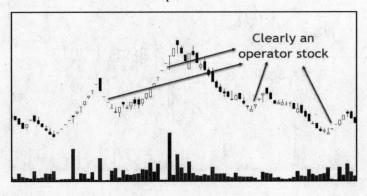

Image 2.3 – Price action is not smooth (Example 3)

If you look at Image 2.3, it has too many gaps and no activity on many trading days. It clearly shows that some operators are controlling this stock. It's better to avoid such scripts.

I don't want to fill this book with too many such useless charts. I hope this information is clear. If you get confused when you see a chart, you can always move on to other scripts as there is no rule to trade solely in that particular script.

What Is a Trend Line?

A **trend line** is a straight line drawn on a chart by connecting two or more price peaks. It reveals the trend of the script and support and resistance points, and allows you to spot any excellent trade opportunities.

A trend line speaks more than words do!

Here are some useful references for drawing a trend line:

- Price peaks

- The slope of the trend line

In addition, the price should respect the trend line.

We need to consider 6-month to 1-year duration charts for this system as our maximum holding period is just 2 weeks. We do not need to know what happened beyond one year ago as our holding period is shorter than that. Besides, our stop-loss management process will take care of any impact of crucial price points which occurred more than a year ago.

Price Peaks

A minimum of 2 peaks need to be connected for a trend line to be considered valid.

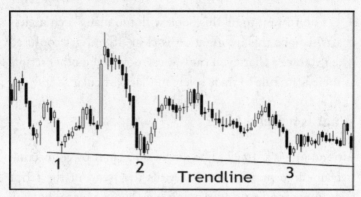

Image 2.4 – A support trend line (Example)

Image 2.4 shows an example of a trend line that connects 3 peaks. It can also be called a **support trend line**.

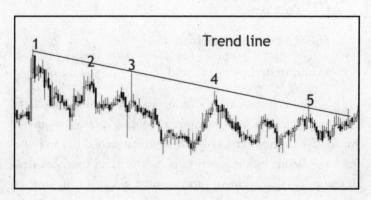

Image 2.5 - A resistance trend line (Example)

Image 2.5 shows another example of a trend line that connects 5 peaks. It can also be called a **resistance trend line**.

A trend line can be considered a **powerful trend line** when it connects a larger number of peaks.

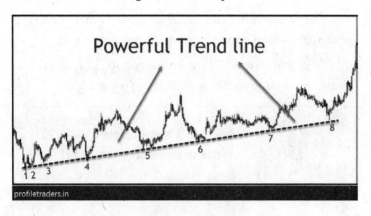

Image 2.6 – A powerful trend line (Example)

The trend line drawn in Image 2.6 is potent, as it connects 8 peaks.

We should note that when a price shows a decisive break of the trend line, it will make a large and rapid movement on the opposite side.

The Slope of the Trend Line

Ideally, the trend line that shows less than the medium slope (less than 45 degrees) is the safer bet, because this is the sign of a healthy trend.

As the slope of a trend line increases, the validity of the support or resistance level decreases.

A steep trend line results from a sharp advance (or decline) over a brief period.

The trend line created from such quick moves is unlikely to offer a strong support or resistance level.

Even if the trend line is connected to 3 or more valid points, attempting to take a trade is not a good idea.

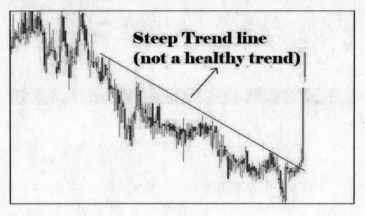

Image 2.7 – A steep trend line (Example)

Image 2.7 shows an example of a steep trend line.

It is not a healthy sign, and this script is most likely the victim of operators.

The Price Should Respect the Trend Line

Whenever you draw a trend line, ensure that the price respects the trend line with all its peaks.

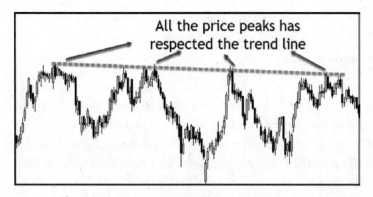

Image 2.8 – A trend line respected by many peaks

Image 2.8 shows a trend line that is respected by all the peaks of the price. Hence, this is a powerful trend line.

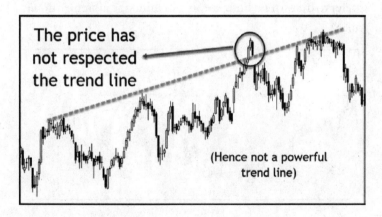

Image 2.9 – A trend line which is not respected by all the peaks

Image 2.9 shows a trend line that is not respected by all the peaks of the price. Hence, this is a not powerful trend line.

Always remember that drawing a trend line is subjective and an art form. Don't get into arguments or discussions with anyone over a trend line. Remember the guidelines mentioned earlier whenever you try to draw one.

In this book, I am willing to provide more emphasis only on the resistance trend line in Section 1, as this book is designed for retail traders who start out with small capital. Due to their low capital, they can only afford to take their breakout trades in equities. Taking trades in futures requires significant capital as per money management rules (which I am going to explain later), so they will not be able to opt for short trades.

I will show some charts below just to indicate how I prefer to draw trend lines keeping in mind the aforementioned rules.

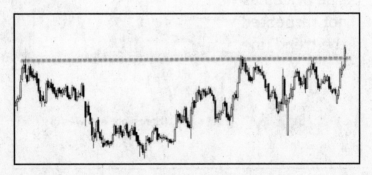

Image 2.10 – A breakout (Example 1)

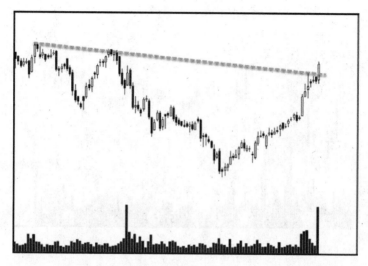

Image 2.11 – A breakout (Example 2)

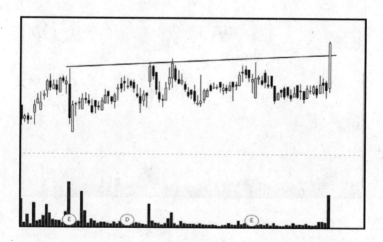

Image 2.12 – A breakout (Example 3)

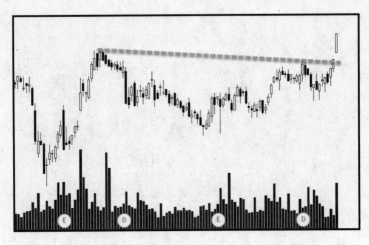

Image 2.13 – A breakout (Example 4)

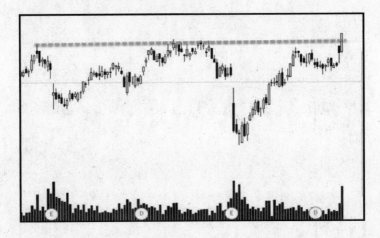

Image 2.14 – A breakout (Example 5)

By this time, you should have some clarity on what kind of scripts you are looking for and how to draw solid trend lines.

Summary

- We only look at daily charts with a 6-month to 1-year duration when drawing a trend line.

- We don't consider charts that don't have a smooth price action.

- When a trend line connects more peaks, it becomes a dominant trend line, and the break of such a trend line results in big movements.

- The slope of the trend line should be less than 45 degrees.

- The price should respect the trend line at all its peaks.

- Drawing trend lines is an art, and it's subjective. So there is no need to debate over them with anyone.

3

How to Identify a Genuine Breakout in 60 Seconds

A traditional breakout trading technique is to enter a long trade whenever the price breaks the resistance trend line along with volumes, or when the current candle closes above the trend line.

This idea looks great in theory, but in reality it's difficult to get good results. Let's take a look at some charts.

Image 3.1 – Breakout or false breakout? (Example 1)

If you look at Image 3.1, the price has closed above the resistance trend line. Do you think it's a genuine breakout?

Don't forget we are ignoring the big selling wick on the breakout candle (the big upper shadow). What this indicates is that selling is strong (probably from smart money) at the current price level.

Until the price negates this selling, it cannot go up, and it requires some time to neutralize this selling. Hence the probability of a false breakout is very high.

You can see the result in Image 3.2.

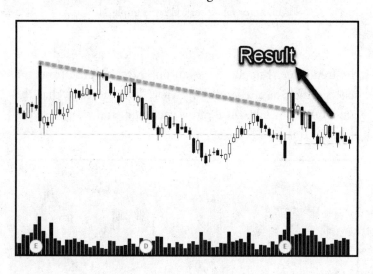

Image 3.2 – Breakout or false breakout? (Example 1 result)

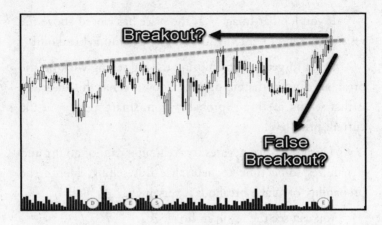

Image 3.3 – Breakout or false breakout? (Example 2)

Once again, in Image 3.3, the price has closed above the trend line. But there was an opposite response from the sellers which resulted in a big wick. This indicates that the probability of a false breakout is very high, and we can see the result in Image 3.4.

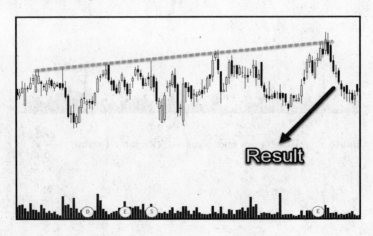

3.4 – Breakout or false breakout? (Example 2 result)

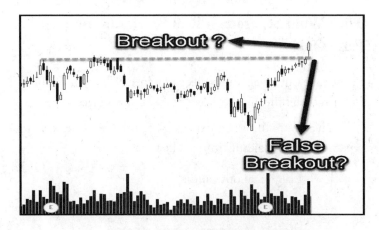

Image 3.5 – Breakout or false breakout? (Example 3)

Once again, an example is shown in Image 3.5 where the price has closed above the trend line. But there is an opposite response from the sellers, which resulted in a big wick. It indicates that the probability of a false breakout is very high, and we can see the result in Image 3.6.

Image 3.6 – Breakout or false breakout? (Example 3 result)

Then What Separates a Real Breakout From a False One?

Please take out a pen and a piece of paper. What you're about to learn is significant and needs to be immortalized.

The four things mentioned below are essential to separate a real breakout from a fake one:

1. A big breakout candle

2. Short time

3. Absence of opposite party response

4. Good volume

Don't make any conclusion as of now. Please read both this chapter and the next one (which covers the execution aspects) completely and with an open mind, and then feel free to take a call.

A Big Breakout Candle

As the name suggests, the breakout should happen with a big candle, because the involvement of smart money at crucial price levels (in our case, near or at the resistance trend line) will always result in a big move.

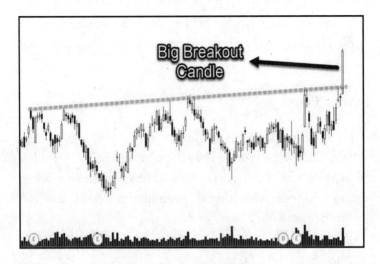

Image 3.7 – A big breakout candle (Example 1)

Image 3.8 – A big breakout candle (Example 2)

If you look at Images 3.7 and 3.8, a breakout happened with a big candle compared to the average candle size in that particular script.

Short Time

I have included this parameter to filter out the fake ones. Often, traders consider a few scripts in which the price has moved outside of the resistance trend line with small candles. It often happens when they draw an invalid trend line or less powerful trend line.

In this system, we always refer to the daily chart. Hence, the breakout should happen in one single day. We don't consider the scripts which will display a small range of candles after breaking the resistance trend line. That doesn't

mean such scripts will not make a big move, just that they are outside the scope of this system. Remember, no one will be able to catch all the big moves!

You should have a system with a clear definition, and while using such a system, you should be able to take trades with fewer emotions.

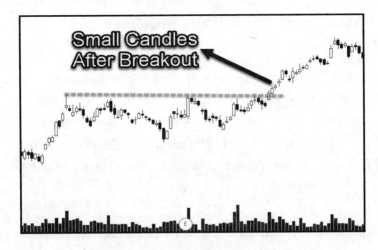

Image 3.9 – A failure of the short time concept (Example 1)

Image 3.10 – A failure of the short time concept (Example 2)

Images 3.9 and 3.10 show examples in which the price has displayed small candles after breaking above the resistance trend line. We should avoid such scripts.

Absence of Opposite Party Response

This exceptional quality stands out from the traditional breakout trading concept. As we look for the breakout of the resistance trend line, if it is a genuine breakout, sellers should be absent or smart money is keen to absorb any selling!

It means we don't like to see a big selling wick on the breakout candle because it indicates the presence of some serious selling.

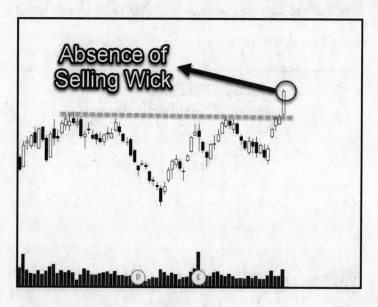

Image 3.11 – Absence of a selling wick (Example 1)

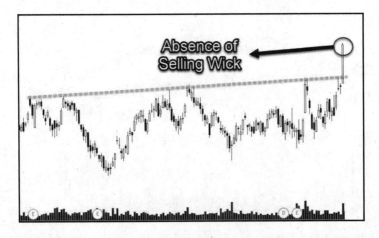

Image 3.12 – Absence of a selling wick (Example 2)

Image 3.11 shows the complete absence of a selling wick, which clearly indicates the intentions of smart money.

Image 3.12 shows the presence of a slight selling wick. It is acceptable since the selling wick size is almost negligible compared to the size of the candle

You can use common sense to decide this. If you need a specific reference, then you can remember that the selling wick should be less than 20% of the entire body of the candle.

For example, if the day's low is 100 and the day's high is 110, then the day's close should have been above 108 (the day's range is 10 points and 20% of the day's range is 2 points).

Image 3.13 – Presence of a selling wick (Example 1) – not suitable for a breakout

Image 3.13 displays a considerable amount of selling wick on the breakout candle. Hence, it's not a pick under our breakout trading system.

Image 3.14 – Presence of a selling wick (Example 2) – not suitable for a breakout

Image 3.14 also displays a considerable amount of selling wick on the breakout candle. Hence, it's not a pick under our breakout trading system.

Good Volume

It is easy to understand and essential to get the confirmation that smart money is involved in the breakout scenario.

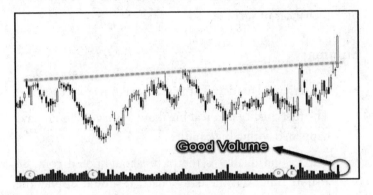

Image 3.15 – Good volume (Example 1)

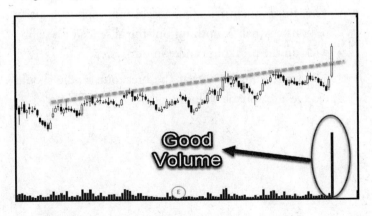

Image 3.16 – Good volume (Example 2)

If you look at Images 3.15 and 3.16, the breakout candle has received a good volume spike, which indicates the involvement of smart money.

Please note, it's always a good idea to pick scripts which show some days of consolidation before the breakout. It gives an opportunity for sellers and indicates shorts build-up. The breakout on the upside indicates that sellers have failed, and they are now running for cover. These kinds of scripts have higher chances of success.

Summary

- It is essential to identify the real breakouts to get success.

- The first quality of a real breakout is that it should have happened with a big candle.

- The second quality is that a breakout should come in a short time. On the daily chart, it should display the breakout criteria in one day.

- The third quality is the absence of opposite party response, which is nothing but the absence of a selling wick on the breakout candle in our system.

- The fourth quality is that the breakout candle should receive a reasonable volume.

4

Execution Matters a Lot in Trading

If you intend to win a game, then you should know all the rules of the game in advance. Then only you can plan and show your talent in the live game.

From the traders' perspective, this is called a trade plan. Plenty of successful traders give the utmost significance to the **trade plan**.

Before entering any trade, you should know, at bare minimum, the five aspects below.

1.   Based on your system, where is your entry point?

2.   In case your analysis goes wrong or your trade setup fails, where is your stop-loss?

3.   Where is your anticipated exit, based on your system to book the profits?

4.   What is the amount you are risking on this particular trade?

5.   How much do you risk on this trade out of your entire portfolio?

Answering these questions every time before you make a trade can help you plan your trades better.

The aforementioned trade plan applies to all types of trading.

Let's discuss how to define this plan for our breakout trading system.

Entry-Stop Loss-Target

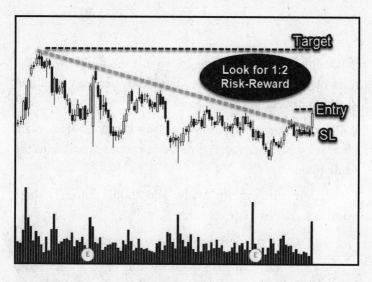

Image 4.1 – Entry-stop loss-target criteria in a breakout trading system during a down trend

As shown in Image 4.1, the entry should come just a few ticks above the high of the breakout candle.

Stop-loss will be a few ticks below the low of the breakout candle.

This script is showing a breakout from a downtrend, so you can aim at the beginning of the trend line or the topmost swing as the target.

Only opt to take the trade if it shows a minimum of a 1:2 risk/reward ratio. Otherwise, you need to ignore the setup and look for better trade setups.

Note: Entry should only come above the high of the breakout candle. Never buy below the high of the breakout candle. Also, avoid the trade if it opens above 2% from the previous day's high, as it increases the stop-loss points and also might attract profit booking. Don't buy even if it opens above 2% and comes back to the previous day's high, because it's against the breakout concept.

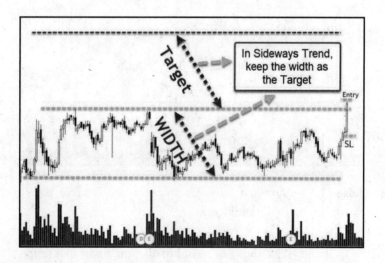

Image 4.2 – Entry-stop loss-target criteria in the breakout trading system during a sideways trend

As shown in Image 4.2, the entry should come just a few ticks above the high of the breakout candle.

The stop-loss will be a few ticks below the low of the breakout candle.

This script shows a breakout from a sideways trend, so you can aim for the same width of the sideways trend as the target.

Only opt to take the trade if it shows a minimum of a 1:2 risk/reward ratio. Otherwise, you need to ignore the setup and look for better trade setups.

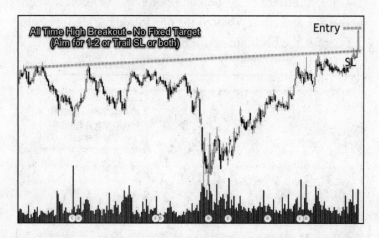

Image 4.3 – Entry-stop loss-target criteria in the breakout trading system during an all-time high

Image 4.3 shows a breakout of all-time highs in a script. In this case, it's tough to come up with a fixed target, as we don't have any reference points on the upside.

One can plan to book profits at a 1:2 risk/reward ratio, or trail stop-loss below every swing low (you never know how far it will go!).

Besides, one can also plan a partial exit at a 1:2 risk/ reward ratio, and manage the remaining position with the concept of a trail SL.

The Untold Story of Trail SL

It is the most crucial aspect of this trading system. This concept is also missing in most other trading systems. Read this section a few times until it gets into your subconscious mind.

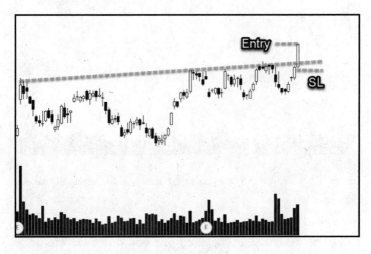

Image 4.4 – A breakout trade (Example 1)

If you look at Image 4.4, we have a clear breakout trade.

- Breakout candle is big ✓ ☐
- Short time ✓ ☐

- Absence of a selling wick ✓ ☐

- Good volume ✓ ☐

It satisfies all our criteria. Hence, we will place a buy order tomorrow above the high of the breakout candle. If triggered, the stop-loss will be below the low of the breakout candlee.

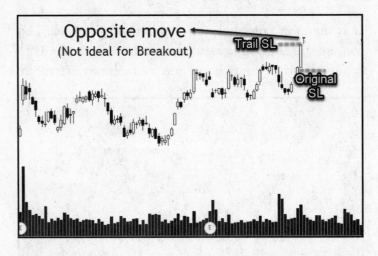

Image 4.5 – Trail SL in the case of a small candle after a breakout (Example 1)

The next day, it triggered our buy order (as the price traded above the high of the breakout candle).).

However, it failed to make a big move on the upside.

Remember, our criteria for a breakout is that the price should make a big move in a short time and in the absence of selling.

The breakout rule applies for the next 2-3 trading sessions after the breakout (as smart money will act, either through selling, buying more, or doing nothing).

*If they **buy** – the price will **go up**.*

*If they **don't react** – the price will **go up**, or it will **stay there** (but selling will not occur).*

*If they **sell** – the price will show **selling** or a **fall**.*

But in the above case, **we can see evident selling on the day after the breakout.**

Hence, it doesn't make any sense to retain the original stop-loss. It is better to trail below the low of the current day's candle, as shown in Image 4.5.

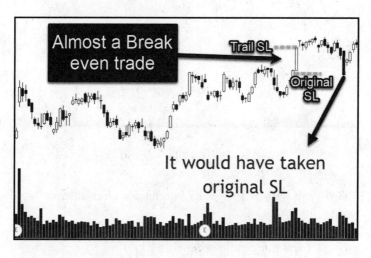

Image 4.6 – Result in the case of a small candle after a breakout (Example 1)

This action of trail SL **resulted in a breakeven trade (with maybe the loss of a few points). But it saved 90% of the initial risk amount.**

Note: Sometimes, the price will hit your trail SL and then reach your target. You should not change the trail SL concept just because of this. The idea of this system is to reduce the initial risk as much as possible if the price shows any danger, and to ride the profits with clear breakout scripts.

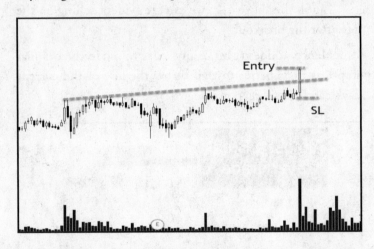

Image 4.7 – A breakout trade (Example 22)

If you look at Image 4.7, we have a clear all-time high breakout trade.

- Breakout candle is big ✔ ☐
- Short time ✔ ☐
- Absence of a selling wick ✔ ☐
- Good volume ✔ ☐

It satisfies all our criteria. Hence, we will place a buy order tomorrow above the high of the breakout candle. If triggered, the stop-loss will be below the low of the breakout candle.

Image 4.8 – Trail SL in the case of a small candle after a breakout (Example 2)

The next day, it triggered our buy order (as the price traded above the high of the breakout candle).).

However, it failed to make a big move on the upside and resulted in a doji candle.

Remember, our criteria for a breakout is that the price should make a big move in a short time and in the absence of selling.

Hence, it doesn't make any sense to retain the original stop-loss. **It is better to trail below the low of the current day's candle,** as shown in Image 4.8.

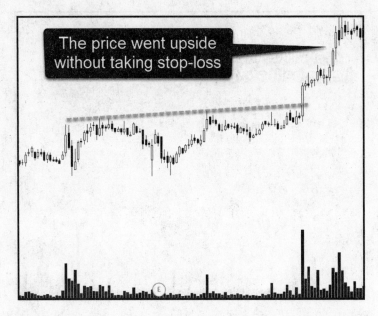

The price went upside without taking stop-loss

Image 4.9 – Result in the case of a small candle after a breakout (Example 2)

However, this time price didn't hit the trail SL and went upside.

In the worst-case scenario, the smart money will show their reaction within 2-3 days after the breakout. In this way, we reduce the initial risk!

Now we will look at one more example.

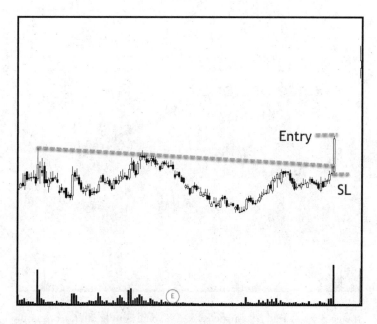

Image 4.10 – A breakout trade (Example 2)

If you look at Image 4.10, we have a clear all-time high breakout trade.

- Breakout candle is big ✓ ☐
- Short time ✓ ☐
- Absence of a selling wick ✓ ☐
- Good volume ✓ ☐

It satisfies all our criteria. Hence, we will place a buy order tomorrow above the high of the breakout candle. If triggered, the stop-loss will be below the low of the breakout candle.

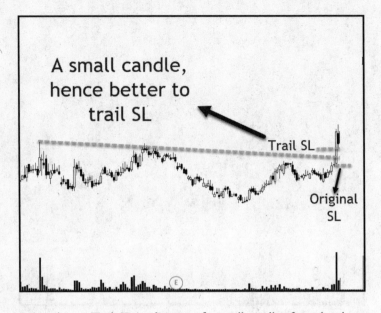

Image 4.11 – Trail SL in the case of a small candle after a breakout (Example 3)

The next day, it triggered our buy order (as the price traded above the high of the breakout candle).

However, it moved only a little bit on the upside and resulted in a small bearish candle.

Remember, our criteria for a breakout is that the price should make a big move in a short time and in the absence of selling.

Hence, it doesn't make any sense to retain the original stop-loss. It is better to trail below the low of the current day's candle, as shown in Image 4.11.

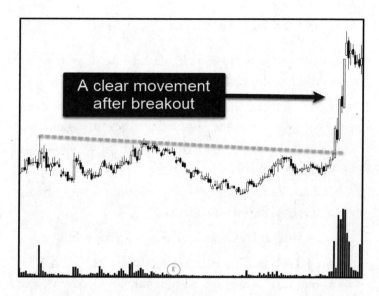

Image 4.12 – Result in the case of a small candle after breakout (Example 3)

This time, again, the price didn't hit the trail SL and went upside immediately.

Note: I can give many examples of this concept. However, I feel that these three scenarios are enough to convey what I am trying to say!

After showing a breakout, the price rarely witnesses significant selling. In most cases, it will rally on the upside immediately or go sideways and then rally on the upside or slow down, and then it will fall.

I am trying to minimize our losses by 75-90% if it fails to make a big move on the upside.

How To Take Your Exit to the Next Level

I repeat: only entry and exit decide the fate of your trade, irrespective of your reputation, experience, or qualifications!

I have noticed that many traders quickly learn about entry, but when it comes to exiting, they struggle a lot. Because every time, the exit will tell you whether you made a profit or a loss.

In both cases, it triggers many emotions, so you should have a proper plan toward your exit.

I can suggest two steps for managing your exit:

Step 1: As per the plan (Images 4.1, 4.2, and 4.3 for a downtrend, sideways, and all-time high, respectively), exit 100% of the position at the target level.

Follow the steps below for a few months until you can manage your existing trades. This method involves many activities :

- Search for breakout scripts every day.

- Shortlist only 2-3 scripts for the next day. Don't try to keep more than 3 scripts on any trading day.

- The next day, when the market opens, place an SL-M buy order above the high of the breakout candle for all the scripts.

- If it opens with a small gap (less than 2%), then you can buy at market order.

- If you bought any, keep a stop-loss order below the low of the breakout candle.

- Again, search for breakout scripts after market hours.

- The next day, once the market opens, keep a stop-loss for your existing positions.

- Then you can place an SL-M buy order for any new scripts.

- If you get a small candle or a selling candle after the breakout, trail your SL from the low of the breakout candle to the low of the next day's candle (Images 4.4 to 4.12).

- When the price reaches your target, either exit manually or place a limit sell order to close the position at the target level.

- Maintain a trading journal. Write all your trades here. Analyze the failed trades.

- Repeat the entire process.

Step 2 : Only after you are familiar with the above process should you plan to implement this step. It contains all the procedures that are mentioned in Step 1.

The only new thing is that instead of exiting 100% of the position at the target, exit only 75%. Carry the remaining 25% with a trail stop-loss below the low of the target day's candle or below any swing loww.

Many times, these breakout scripts run like crazy, and 25% of the position in one such trade has the potential to absorb the loss of 25 of your trades!

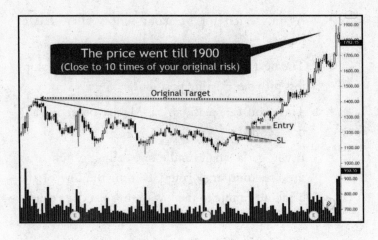

Image 4.13 – Partial exit (Example 1)

Image 4.13 explains everything about the power of partial exits. You will make an excellent profit if you keep using the trail SL concept below the low of every swing.

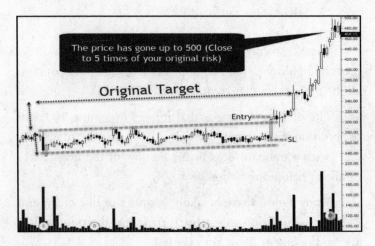

Image 4.14 – Partial exit (Example 2)

Image 4.14 explains the same story of partial exits. It would have given 5-6 times the returns of your original risk for your 25% position.

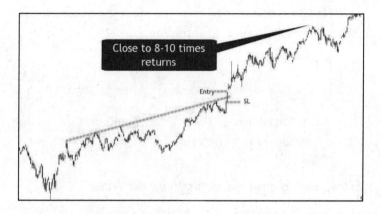

Image 4.15 – Partial exit (Example 3)

Image 4.15 explains another story of partial exits. It would have given 8-10 times the returns of your original risk for your 25% position.

I hope that after seeing these examples you understand the power of partial exits

How I Stopped Losing Money Trading

I am now going to reveal some shocking news to all of you.

Whatever you have learned until now is only 10% of what goes into successful trading! Were you shocked to hear that?

Well, that's a solid fact!

Anybody can come with a trading system that has fair efficiency and a good risk/reward ratio; in fact, you can find so many such trading systems by searching for them onlinee.

However, risk management or money management is the primary key to successful trading.

It raises two critical questions:

How much should you deploy/risk per trade?

What percentage of the capital should you deploy in trades at any given time?

How much should you deploy/risk per trade?

I suggest a simple technique for this. For any one trade, use only 10% of your capital, irrespective of the risk.

For example, let's say you have ₹1,00,000 as your capital and you finalize script ABC. Assume your entry price is ₹100. Then 10% of your capital is ₹10,000, so you can buy 10,000/100 = 100 shares.

Using this approach, your entire capital percentage risk per trade varies between 0.5%-2% (based on how deep your stop-loss is), which is fine.

Some people recommend risking only 1-2% of your capital per trade, and they don't put an upper cap on the capital. This causes some confusion, and you will not be able to opt for more trades.

Let me explain with an example. Assume your capital is ₹1,00,000.

You are planning to risk 2% of your capital per trade, which is ₹2000/trade. You have shortlisted script XYZ. The entry is at ₹1000 and the SL is at ₹990.

Then the total number of shares to buy = ₹2000/10 = 200. The capital required to buy the 200 shares = 200 x ₹1000 = ₹2,00,000.

But you don't have ₹2,00,000 capital in your account, do you?

Thus, the simple way is to deploy only 10% of your capital on one trade!

What percentage of the total capital should you deploy in trades at any given time?

This is the million-dollar question!

I feel like no one can answer this question with 100% accuracy or using a formula.

It is effortless to say, "Deploy 100% of your capital in uptrend, only 50% in a sideways trend, and sit with your cash in a downtrend."

However, implementing this is a real problem. I have a simple suggestion for new traders.

Never deploy more than 50% of your capital on trades until you experience all the market trends (like uptrends, sideways trends, downtrends, and random conditions).

In other words, you are not supposed to carry more than 5 trades on any given market conditions (except for the remaining 25% of the position on winning trades, as you have already made a profit with these trades for 75% of the position).

Once you cross this stage, you automatically get the knowledge of how to increase or decrease your allocated capital based on the market conditions.

Why Even Smart People Fall for Market Conditions

When I was working in the software industry, I had a teammate. His name was Suraj (name changed for privacy reasons), and he excelled at whatever he did. He was smart and would come up with brilliant ideas; in fact, he was the one who introduced me to the stock market a decade back.

He was quite an achiever, whether it was in his career or his personal ventures beyond the office. When he jumped into trading, he had a robust system with proper risk management. However, he still failed at trading!

I have spent a couple of years wondering why he failed at trading, and admitted to myself the fact that his failure generated fear in my mind. When even an intelligent person like Suraj failed at trading, what chance did I have?

However, after several years of analysis, I realized the rationale behind his failure, which I will be presenting to create awareness in this session

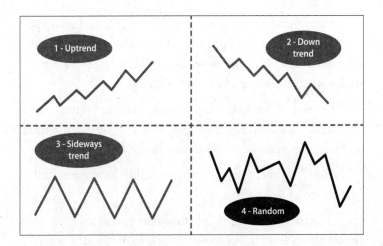

Image 4.16 – The four stages of the market

As shown in Image 4.16, the market has four trends.

Every trading system layout has different results in these four stages.

A trader has to go through all these market conditions with a particular trading system. An excellent trading system can reward better outcomes within 2-3 market stages, as mentioned above.

So, even if a trader uses such an excellent trading system, he should know how to handle the system when the market stage is not in the system's favor. He should learn how to avoid trades (or how to reduce the risk) in such market stages. Otherwise, his learning curve will not become complete.

For example, if you have a trending system, it works well with uptrends and downtrends. It doesn't give more trades and results in a sideways trend and random market conditions.

Suraj made a similar mistake. He initially picked up one trading system backed up by a lot of studies and backtesting. It worked fine for some time, but it did not generate more trades when the market conditions changed.

Instead of sticking to the same trading system, Suraj identified another trading system. It worked for some time, and later the same story repeated. Finally, he gave up!

Now, tell me, do you want to make the same mistake? I hope not!

Thus I am stating in advance that to taste success with the breakout system, you need to stick to the process with the aforementioned four stages of the market.

You may ask me, "How much time do you need to face all the four stages of the market?" My answer is, "I don't know!"

The market is not in my control. Sometimes it shows all these different conditions within a year, and sometimes it takes 3-4 years.

We can aim for approximately 2 years to achieve some success with this breakout trading system.

But I can list some of the features of the breakout system below (keeping only long trades).

In an uptrend, you will get many scripts every day and get good results.

In a sideways trend, you will get a decent number of trades and also get good results.

In a downtrend, you won't get a larger number of

trades. Besides, most trades get out of the trade at a breakeven (recall my trail SL plan in case of a small or selling candle after breakout).

In random market conditions, the result is not guaranteed. On some days, you won't get any trades. Other times, the price will hit your target on the same day. In some cases, you will take a stop-loss.

We should be RIGID about our RULES and FLEXIBLE about our EXPECTATIONS from the market.

But the problem is that we are RIGID about our EXPECTATIONS but FLEXIBLE about our RULES.

Please keep this in mind.

Summary

- Having a trade plan is essential to track all your trades and to achieve success in trading.

- In this system, entry should come above the high of the breakout candle.

- In this system, stop-loss will be below the low of the breakout candle.

- You can target the beginning point of the trend line in a downtrend, and you can target the same width of the trend in a sideways trend or an uptrend with trail stop-loss.

- You should trail your SL when there is a small candle or selling candle immediately after the breakout day.

- After some practice, you can plan to exit only 75% of your position at the target and carry the remaining 25% with the target candle low as the stop-loss.

- Allocate only 10% of your capital per trade.

- If you are a beginner, don't deploy more than 50% of your capital at any given time.

- To taste success, you should follow this system across all four stages of the market.

5

Top 10 Questions and Answers on Breakout Trading

Whenever I explain this system to any group, I get many questions, and most of them are similar. I have listed the top 10 questions along with my answers. I hope this will help you if you share some of the same questions.

Q1) Can we take short trades with this breakout concept?

The straightforward answer is "No".

This trading system is designed specifically for Indian retail traders who have a small capital.

As you know, in Indian market conditions, we can't carry our short trades in equity for the next few days.

To take a positional short trade, we should look at futures or options. Taking a positional short trade in futures or options with a small trade capital is a terrible idea.

So if you are a retail trader with small capital, don't look for short trades using this breakout concept.

Q2) Can we take trades in F&O using this breakout concept?

Again, taking a trade in futures or options is a different ball game from a risk management and volatility perspective.

I suggest avoiding options as you will need to master other factors such as expiry time and volatility factors.

With futures, it depends on your capital. If the allocation is within 10% of your capital per trade, it should be okay.

However, you will have to face two challenges:

1. In a gap down scenario, the percentage risk per trade might vary drastically. In other words, you might lose more money in case of a big gap down open.

2. You may not be able to partially exit at the target (as you might buy only one lot).

Again, if you are a retail trader with small capital, don't look to trade in F&O using this breakout concept

Q3) Can we buy before a breakout candle high?

An analysis is one aspect, and confirmation from the market is another aspect. We should always look for confirmation from the market before initiating our trade.

With this system, the intentions of smart money will only be confirmed when the price breaks the breakout candle high.

Hence, it's not a good idea to initiate a trade before the price breaks the breakout candle high.

Q4) Can we deploy more capital for this concept?

Let's say that you have a friend who doesn't know how to drive even a Maruti Swift, and you just bought a brand new Audi Q3. Your friend insists that he will drive the car. Would you give him the keys? I'm sure you wouldn't even show them to him!

Similarly, even if you have significant capital, start applying this concept with small capital. Once you cross all the four stages of the market with this system and you become confident, you can deploy more money

Q5) Can we take more than 5 trades using this breakout concept?

If you are a beginner, don't deploy more than 50% of your capital at any given time. In other words, you can carry only 5 trades at any point in time.

Once you overcome all four stages of the market with this system, you will automatically how learn to deploy more capital based on market conditions.

Q6) Can I deploy more than 10% of my capital per trade?

Staying in the game is always more crucial than losing everything and exiting the game. Hence, it is not a good idea to deploy more than 10% of your capital on any trade.

Q7) How do I trail SL for this breakout concept?

It is a good question from an execution perspective. You can follow the steps below:

1. Once your buy order above the breakout candle triggers, immediately keep an SL below the low of the breakout candle.

2. The next day after the breakout candle, if you get a small candle, trail SL below the low of that day.

3. If you get another big candle on the upside, you can trail your SL below the low of that candle. In both these cases (2 and 3), it will be a breakeven trade (in most cases), and you don't have to worry about losses (as shown in Image 5.1.).

4. After 2-3 days, if you see significant selling, like a bearish engulfing or a big selling pin bar, then you can trail SL below the low of that candle (as shown in Image 5.2).

5. In all other cases, you can trail SL below the next swing low (please note that you will rarely get the next swing low as the idea of this trading concept is to catch a big, quick move).

6. Once the price reaches near your target, you can exit using a market order or a limit order.

If you want to know more about different types of orders, please refer to this article:

https://www.profiletraders.in/post/what-are-the-different-types-of- orders-which-order-type-is-best

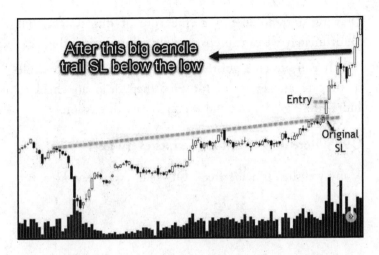

Image 5.1 – Trail SL in the case of a big candle

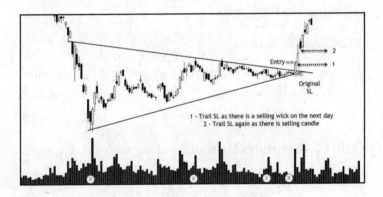

Image 5.2 – Trail SL in the case of a selling candle

Q8) Is there any mechanism to scan the scripts for this system?

Unfortunately not!

Drawing a trend line is at the core of this system, but unfortunately we can't prepare an algorithm for trend lines.

If you are an algorithm expert and think it's possible to prepare an algorithm for this, then drop an email to Indrazith.s@gmail.com and we can have a discussion.

Q9) Where do I check for scripts every day?

Many websites provide free EOD data every day. Here are some:

https://in.tradingview.com/

https://chartink.com/

https://in.investing.com/

https://www.icharts.in/

I prefer to use https://in.tradingview.com/ as this site is more user-friendly. If you noticed, all the images used in this book have been taken from Trading View.

Q10) Can I try intraday trading along with this concept?

It's always difficult to ride two boats at a time! My suggestion is to try one concept first.

Even if you show good progress with this system, you might lose your focus and balance of mind if you sustain losses while intraday trading.

Ultimately, the choice is yours!

Section 2

Intraday Trading

1

Read This Before You Jump into Intraday Trading

Is Intraday Trading Just Gambling?

Intraday trading is my favorite type of trading. I have deployed many algorithmic (both directional and non-directional) systems while writing this information, but I always get a sense of satisfaction when I take up a discretionary breakout trade which provides some profits.

Many people argue that intraday trading is risky and equivalent to gambling. I don't completely agree with this statement. Let's take the example of a knife. Do you think it is dangerous? Again, it depends on how you use it. You could use it to chop vegetables with which you could prepare an excellent dish, or you could stab someone with it and cause them injury. In both cases, the knife remains the same, doesn't it?

Similarly, intraday trading is a type of trading that provides fantastic opportunities to the traders for making quick money (compared to swing trading and investments), but it comes with some extra costs.

Let me explain what I mean with a simple example.

Let's say you have to travel from Bangalore to Hyderabad for some work. The distance between Bangalore to Hyderabad is 500 km. You have three options:

Driver ABC drives at an average of 50 km/h, and so he requires 10 hours to reach the destination.

Driver XYZ drives at an average of 80 km/h, and so he requires 6.25 hours to reach the destination.

Driver III drives at an average of 100 km/h, and so he requires 5 hours to reach the destination.

(All of these times are ignoring any breaks in between.)

Now, which driver would you choose?

Most of you would go for driver III because a speed of 100 km/h on a national highway is manageable.

But guess which driver among the three would be more prone to accidents? It's definitely Driver III. Would you still prefer to go with him?

However, this doesn't mean that drivers ABC and XYZ are completely accident-proof drivers. Anything could happen at any moment in life. Driver III just carries a little extra risk since he's driving at a higher speed. But if we take some precautions (like using a well-built car with airbags), this risk can be negated to some extent.

The same logic applies to intraday trading.

Intraday trading is simply a system that offers more opportunities to traders. Naturally, it comes with some noise and a slightly higher failure rate. Anyone can taste success by intraday trading if they learn how to mitigate these risks (through money management rules and by avoiding revenge trading).

Why do many people fail at intraday trading?

Again, this is a debatable topic. There is not a shred of evidence to show that only intraday traders lose money in the market.

I agree that indeed more traders lose money in general, but I feel this is pretty common in all areas of life. You can ask someone who started a start-up, a cricketer, a footballer, a filmmaker, etc. Success only knocks on the doors of those who turn up every day and are persistent, and this also applies to intraday trading.

I don't usually prefer driving through cities, but I love to go down highways and empty roads surrounded by nature.

One day, I was in a situation where I had to drive through Bangalore. After finishing all my work, I was heading back to my place. It was around 3:00 p.m., and I hadn't had breakfast or lunch yet. Naturally, I was hungry, and I was looking for a place to eat some good food. I found a small hotel on the Outer Ring Road run by a family and ordered my lunch.

While eating my quite tasty lunch, I noticed the owner behaving in a strange manner. He was sitting by the entrance of the hotel and throwing stones at any street dogs that happened to come nearby.

I asked him why he was doing that, since the dogs weren't harming him in any way. He said that some customers didn't like the presence of dogs. As I was the only customer at the time, I asked him not to throw any stones since I didn't have any problem with them.

The owner was a little surprised, but agreed to my request. A few minutes later, a little girl came out and started playing with the owner.

She was lovely, and must have been 1.5 or 2 years old. I thought she must have been his daughter. They were having fun, and I also interacted with them occasionally.

Suddenly, the little girl picked up a stone and threw it toward her dad's Omni (a small car used mainly by small business owners to carry luggage in India). Luckily, it didn't do any damage except for making a small dent in the door.

The owner was shocked. He scolded the child and hit her twice. Then his wife emerged from inside and took away the crying kid.

I looked him in the eye. It was clear that he felt more pain because he hit his daughter than because of the dent in his car.

I said to him, **"If you don't mind, may I give you a suggestion?"** He replied, "Sure, sir."

I said**, "Kids don't usually pay attention to what we say, but they imitate our actions unconsciously. You were throwing stones at the dogs. Your daughter is close to you, so she mimicked the same habit. Do you think she learned to throw stones the moment she was born?"**

He was quiet for some time. After a few minutes, his eyes were wet. He said that he would be careful with his behavior, especially in front of his kid, and thanked me for the great lesson.

"You are the average of the five people you spend the most time with." - Jim Rohn

In one of his speeches, the world-famous motivational speaker Jim Rohn delivered the above statement. When it comes to human relationships, we are easily influenced (whether we like it or not) by those who are close to us.

If you want to become a successful intraday trader, it is better to avoid the people who think intraday trading doesn't work or who consider intraday trading gambling.

Instead, you can read good books on intraday trading and follow successful intraday traders, watch their videos, and try to pick their brains by interacting with them whenever you get the chance.

Unpardonable Mistakes Committed by Intraday Traders

I have over a decade of experience with intraday trading. I have seen many people who lost their entire capital, or most of it, in one trading day (or within 2-3 trading days). But I have never seen even a single intraday trader who lost their entire capital over 100 intraday trades.

In simple terms, if you don't lose a significant portion of your capital even after 100 intraday trades, then there is a high probability of you achieving success in intraday trading. The percentage returns depend upon the individual and their trading system. Still, people will have a strong foundation if they don't lose most of their wealth in their first 100 intraday trades.

Most people commit a few terrible mistakes at the beginning of their intraday career and lose their money. Let's take a look at those mistakes:

1. Greediness

Everyone wants to make quick money, but there is a threshold limit for everything. In the previous example, what happens if a person aims to cover the distance between Bangalore to Hyderabad (500 km) in just 3 hours? He will have to drive at an average speed of 167 km/h, which is risky on Indian highways.

On the same note, aiming to earn several million in one trading day also brings more risk to the table. Once in a while, a trader can make good profits in a single trading day, but replicating the same trade by taking more risk on the capital is not a good idea.

Many people risk 20-25% of their capital in one trade when they succeed with some trades. It is not a good idea because the market may give unexpected results anytime, and 2-3 such trades will wipe out your entire capital.

Hence it is always sensible to risk only 2-3% of your capital per trade. This way, even if you get 5 successive failed trades, you don't lose more than 10- 15% of your trading capital. Similarly, ensure you don't lose more than 10% of your trading capital on any trading day, as this will help you to stay in business.

2. Revenge Trading

Revenge trading has been identified as one of the significant causes of failure.

It happens before you've had a chance to think about your next move, and it often leads right back into more bad trades because you're trying too hard just to get even right away – without devoting any time to assessing your previous strategies!

This is one of the classic examples that illustrates how our upbringing can negatively impact our career in general. If a person fails to identify and rectify their issues, they will end up paying a heavy price.

Most parents advise their kids not to fail at their studies, and they insist that their kids should score more marks. In this process, they also indirectly convey the idea that failure is a horrible thing. But when it comes to trading, nobody can achieve a 100% success rate with their trades. Whenever we face some losses in trading, we unconsciously react to correct them by taking more unnecessary trades, and this happens to be the root cause of revenge trading.

To avoid revenge trading, either take your trades consciously or make a rule of not taking more than 3 trades on any trading day.

3. Eagerness to Trade Every Day

This is quite common with most beginners. When you trade on a certain day, it's essential to be aware of the market conditions. If they do not present any direction for several hours, then there can never really be any momentum behind your trades. Thus, unnecessary trades and revenge trades may turn out to be worse than expected because these will result in further losses.

Hence, you need to be constantly aware of the market conditions and plan your trades only when the market is showing favorable conditions for your trading system.

2

How to Analyze Market Sentiment in 5 Minutes?

Most retail traders don't understand the big players' problems. In most cases, retail traders don't come across slippage, but it is a big issue for big players. Orders of retail traders can be fulfilled easily with a slight price difference, but big players can't punch in all their quantities in one order. Therefore, they play an intelligent game when the price fluctuates near support and resistance levels to fill their quantities.

In order to counter the big players' tactics, it is necessary to know what they are doing at different time intervals. We can use market sentiment to understand their actions and plan better trades. There are many variations for arriving at the market sentiment, but I have designed my own, and it is highly beneficial in intraday trading.

When it comes to analyzing market sentiment and knowing whether the trading activity is bullish or bearish for any given day, the market offers immense challenges to traders. Unfortunately, many people think they know what's going on by following majority prospects since everyone else seems to be very confident. In reality, that doesn't always end up working out well, as you'll soon find yourself losing money day trading.

This explanation of 'market sentiment' measures the activities of all these big players from 3 different dimensions. All you need is a simple price chart to perform this analysis.

Please note that you should conduct this analysis after the market closes. You can keep the bullish or bearish behavior of the market sentiment in mind when taking trades the next day.

The three critical aspects required to calculate market sentiment are:

1. Range shift

2. Range extension

3. Extremes

These features measure the big players' activity from three different dimensions.

Range shift indicates the overall impact of big players on the market.

Range extension indicates the impact of big players 1 hour after the market opening.

Extreme indicates big players' urgency to grab any good opportunities.

Let's dive in to learn more about these concepts.

1. Range Shift

In this case, we compare today's price with the previous day's price range. If today's range is moved upside compared to the previous day's range, then we can mark it as positive (Image 2.1).

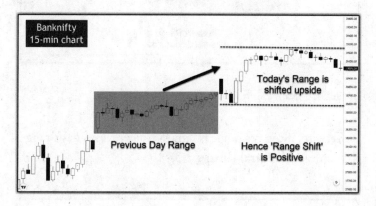

Image 2.1 – Range shift is positive

But if today's range is moved downside compared to the previous day's range, then we can mark it as **negative** (Image 2.2).

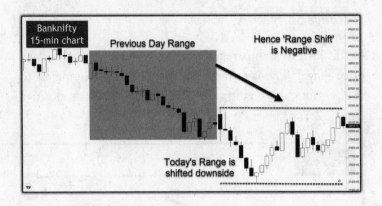

Image 2.2 – Range shift is negative

Otherwise, if today's range is same as the previous day's range, we mark it as **neutral** (Image 2.3).

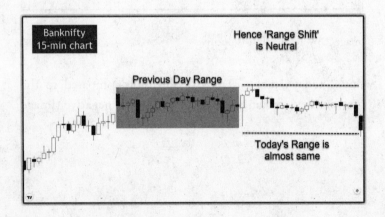

Image 2.3 – Range shift is neutral

This is how we arrive at the first parameter.

2. Range Extension

There is a famous saying in the market:

"Amateurs open the market, and professionals close the market."

It means that most retail traders are eager to trade every day and so they participate immediately when the market opens.

However, expert traders wait for some time, observe the market, and make calculated moves.

This is nothing but range extension. It is a movement of price outside the first 1-hour range of the market.

Range extension is always created by big players who can provide magnitude and direction.

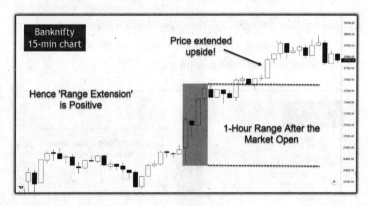

Image 2.4 – Range extension is positive

We consider only today's price action to assess the range extension parameter. In Image 2.4, the first 1-hour range (after the market opens) is highlighted.

The price broke the 1-hour range (the 9th candle) on the upside and extended on the upside, so we can mark the range extension parameter as **positive.**

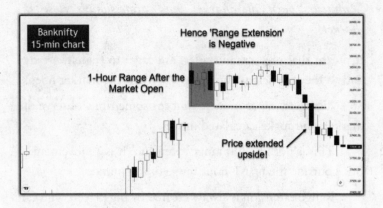

Image 2.5 – Range extension is negative

If you look at Image 2.5, the price has clearly extended the downside, breaking the 1-hour range, so we can mark the range extension parameter as **negative.**

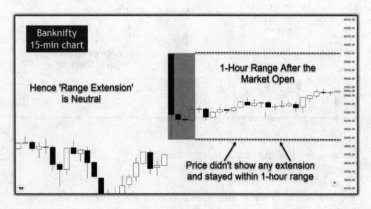

Image 2.6A – Range extension is neutral

If you look at Image 2.6A, the price didn't show any extension and stayed within the 1-hour range for the rest of the day, so we can mark the range extension parameter as **neutral**.

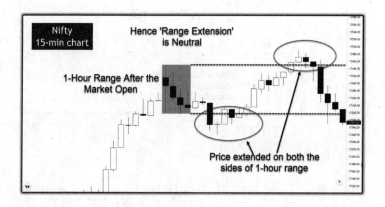

Image 2.6B – Range extension is neutral

If you look at Image 2.6B, the price displayed extension on both sides of the 1-hour range, so even in this case, we can mark the range extension parameter as **neutral**.

3. Extremes

Extremes are nothing but big buying or selling wicks at the day's low or the day's high.

If a candle displays a medium to high buying or selling wick near the day's high or the day's low, then it is considered extreme.

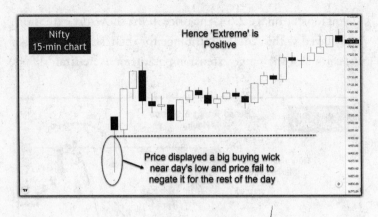

Image 2.7 – Extreme is positive

In Image 2.7, the price displayed a big buying wick near the day's low, and the price failed to negate it for the rest of the day. This shows the power of solid buyers. Hence, we can mark the extreme parameter as **positive**.

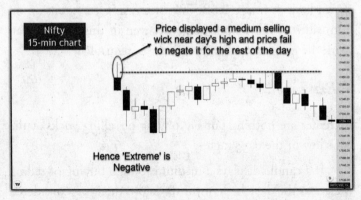

Image 2.8 – Extreme is negative

In Image 2.8, the price displayed a medium selling wick near the day's high, and the price failed to negate it for the rest of the day. This shows the power of strong sellers. Hence, we can mark the extreme parameter as **negative.**

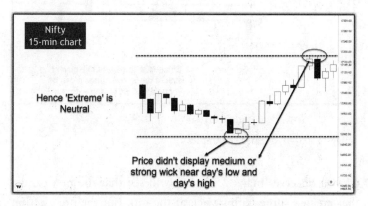

Image 2.9 – Extreme is neutral

In Image 2.9, the price failed to display a medium or strong wick near the day's high or the day's low.

This indicates missing intent from the big players. Hence, we can mark the extreme parameter as neutral.

Please note that while the price can display some wicks in between the price range, we need to consider the wicks near the day's high and the day's low. Besides, the price should not negate those wicks to view it for extreme.

95

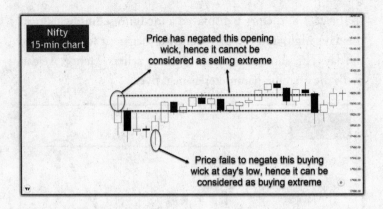

Image 2.10 – Extremes (Examples)

If you observe Image 2.10, you will see that the first candle has created some selling wick at the top. But the price action from the 6th candle has negated (traded in the same range) the impact of the selling wick and has also traded above it. Hence, it cannot be considered a selling wick.

At that exact moment, the 5th candle has some buying wick, the price failed to negate it, and it also comes near the day's low. Hence, the extreme parameter is positive in the above case.

How to Use Market Sentiment

It doesn't matter whether you trade stocks, indices, or crypto. The price action works the same across all the instruments. If you trade in a 24/7 market, then ensure you take a 4-hour range to calculate the range extension parameter. Also, note that you should calculate market sentiment only after the closure of the market.

Example 1

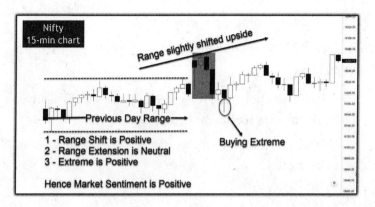

Image 2.11 – Market sentiment calculation

Image 2.11 shows a Nifty 15-minute chart for 12-Jan-2022 and 13-Jan-2022.

Compared to the 12-Jan-2022 price range, on 13-Jan-2022, the price shifted slightly upside, so we can mark the **range shift parameter as positive.**

The 1-hour range on 13-Jan-2022 is highlighted in the black box. The price is not extended above or below the first-hour range (except the buying wick, which we will consider in the extreme parameter), so we can mark the **range extension parameter as neutral.**

There is a decent buying wick near the day's low on 13-Jan-2022, so we can mark the **extreme parameter as positive.**

Market Sentiment:

- Range shift is positive
- Range extension is neutral
- Extreme is positive

Two parameters are positive, and one parameter is neutral. **Thus, the market sentiment is positive.**

So we can look forward to take only long trades on the next trading day.

Example 2

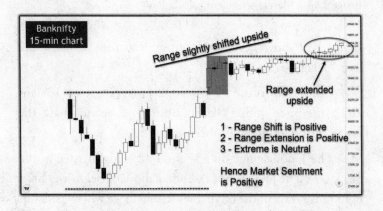

Image 2.12 – Market sentiment calculation

Image 2.12 shows Banknifty 15-minute chart for 8-Feb-2022 and 9-Feb-2022.

Compared to the 8-Feb-2022 price range, on 9-Feb-2022, the price shifted slightly upside. Therefore, we can mark the **range shift parameter as positive.**

The 1-hour range on 9-Feb-2022 is highlighted in the black box. The price is extended slightly on the upside, so we can mark the **range extension parameter as positive.**

It doesn't have a decent buying or selling wick. Here, we can mark the **extreme parameter as neutral.**

Market Sentiment:

- Range shift is positive
- Range extension is positive
- Extreme is neutral

Two parameters are positive, and one parameter is neutral. **Thus, the market sentiment is positive.**

So we can look forward to take only **long trades** on the next trading day.

Example 3

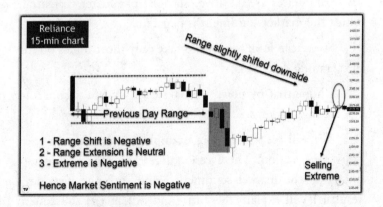

Image 2.13 – Market sentiment calculation

Image 2.13 shows the Reliance 15-minute chart for 10-Feb-2022 and 11-Feb- 2022.

Compared to the 10-Feb-2022 price range, on 11-Feb-2022, the price shifted slightly downside, so we can mark the **range shift parameter as negative.**

The 1-hour range on 11-Feb-2022 is highlighted in the black box. The price didn't show extension on any side. Therefore, we can mark the **range extension parameter as neutral.**

It displayed a decent selling wick near the day's high. Here, we can mark the **extreme parameter as negative.**

Market Sentiment:

- Range shift is negative
- Range extension is neutral
- Extreme is negative

Two parameters are negative, and one parameter is neutral. **Thus, the market sentiment is negative.**

So we can look forward to take only short trades on the next trading day.

I hope that by now, you have clarity when it comes to calculating market sentiment for any trading instrument.

We will see some more examples along with the next day's price action. These case studies are only to illustrate analyzing the market sentiment along with the next day's results. I will explain the entry and exit in the subsequent chapters.

Case Study 1

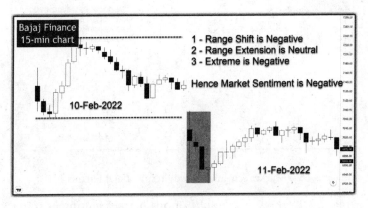

Image 2.14 – Market sentiment study (Bajaj Finance)

Market Sentiment:

- Range shift is negative
- Range extension is neutral
- Extreme is negative

Two parameters are negative, and one parameter is neutral. **Thus, the market sentiment is negative.**

So, we can look forward to take only short trades on the next trading day. Let's see what happened on the next trading day.

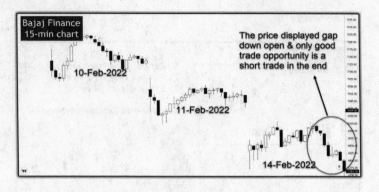

Image 2.15 – Market sentiment study result (Bajaj Finance)

Image 2.15 shows the results of our market sentiment study. On 14-Feb- 2022, the price opened with a big gap down open.

Even if the first candle shows a hammer structure, there is no need to plan a long trade because the market sentiment is negative. The only good tradable intraday move came in the second half, with a significant fall after 1:30 p.m.

Case Study 2

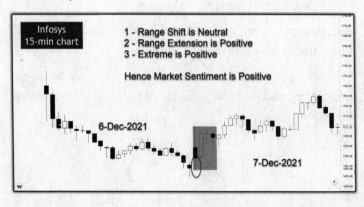

Image 2.16 – Market sentiment study (Infosys)

Market Sentiment:

- Range shift is neutral
- Range extension is positive
- Extreme is positive

Two parameters are positive, and one parameter is neutral. **Hence, the market sentiment is positive.**

So we can look forward to take only **long trades** on the next trading day. Let's see what happened on the next trading day.

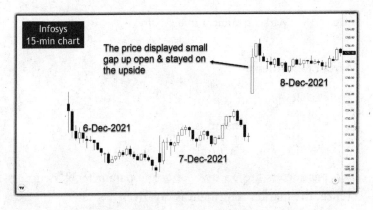

Image 2.17 – Market sentiment study result (Infosys)

Image 2.17 shows the results of our market sentiment study. On 8-Dec-2021, the price opened with a small gap and displayed an open-low formation in the first candle.

The only long trade opportunity is in the first candle, and after showing good movement in the first two candles, it displayed a complete sideways movement for the rest of the day.

Case Study 3

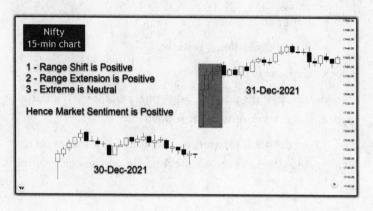

Image 2.18 – Market sentiment study (Nifty)

Market Sentiment:

- Range shift is positive
- Range extension is positive
- Extreme is neutral

Two parameters are positive, and one parameter is neutral. **Hence, the market sentiment is positive.**

So we can look forward to take only **long trades** on the next trading day. Let's see what happened on the next trading day.

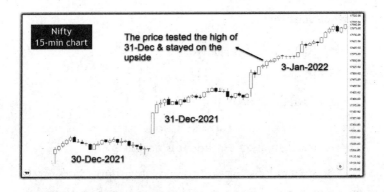

Image 2.19 – Market sentiment study result (Nifty)

Image 2.19 shows the results of our market sentiment study. On 3-Jan-2022, the price opened and tested the high of the previous day. But it showed clear rejection, and buyers pushed the price on the first candle itself.

It trended upside for the rest of the day.

Case Study 4

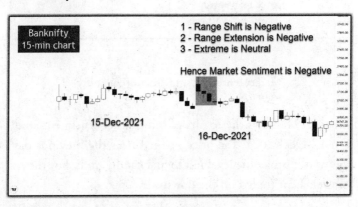

Image 2.20 – Market sentiment study (Banknifty)

Market Sentiment:

- Range shift is negative

- Range extension is negative

- Extreme is neutral

Two parameters are negative, and one parameter is neutral. Therefore, the market sentiment is negative.

So we can look forward to take only short trades on the next trading day. Let's see what happened on the next trading day.

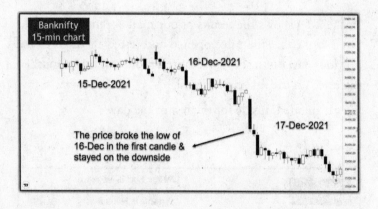

Image 2.21 – Market sentiment study result (Banknifty)

Image 2.21 shows the results of our market sentiment study. On 17-Dec- 2021, the price opened near the previous day's low and it broke the level in the first candle itself. For the rest of the day, it traded on the downside.

Case Study 5

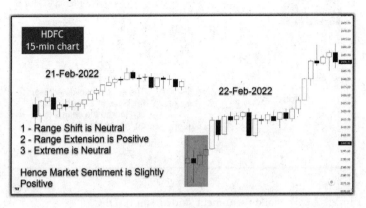

Image 2.22 – Market sentiment study (HDFC)

Market Sentiment:

- Range shift is neutral (because the range expanded from down to top compared to 21-Feb-2022)

- Range extension is positive

- Extreme is neutral (because both buying and selling wicks are present)

Two parameters are neutral, and one parameter is positive. **Thus, the market sentiment is slightly positive.**

It's not advisable to plan trades on the following day, as two neutral parameters highlight the absence of big players.

Let's see what happened on the next trading day.

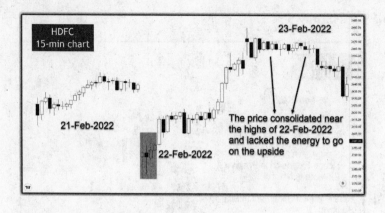

Image 2.23 – Market sentiment study result (HDFC)

Image 2.23 shows the results of our market sentiment study. On 23-Feb- 2022, the price opened near the high of the previous day, but it clearly lacked the energy to go on the upside and witnessed some selling at the end. This was visible on the last market day sentiment with the absence of big players (two parameters are neutral).

Case Study 6

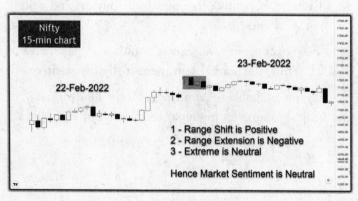

Image 2.24 – Market sentiment study (Nifty)

Market Sentiment:

- Range shift is positive
- Range extension is negative
- Extreme is neutral

One parameter is neutral, one parameter is negative, and one parameter is positive. **Hence, the market sentiment is neutral.**

Let's see what happened on the next trading day.

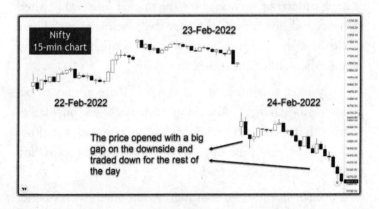

Image 2.25 – Market sentiment study result (Nifty)

Image 2.25 shows the results of our market sentiment study. On 24-Feb- 2022, the price displayed a big gap down open and traded toward the downside for the rest of the day.

The market sentiment didn't work correctly in this case. This example illustrates that market sentiment doesn't work on all days. In fact, don't expect any of the concepts to work well on every single trading day.

Russia invaded Ukraine before the market opened on 24-Feb-2022. Hence, Nifty displayed a big gap down open and fell later. So you should know that any important fundamental change or news can change the market's direction. Money management rules play a crucial role in trading.

Precautions To Follow With Market Sentiment

Estimating the market sentiment is one aspect, but trading in the live market is another. Please do remember that there is a big difference between how the market feels today when it closes and how it feels the next day when it opens. There could be a massive fundamental shift overnight, which can change the market direction completely.

Market sentiment works better if there are no global fundamental changes. Also, don't depend solely on market sentiment to plan your trades. Instead, align it with any other technical concept. I use open types, candlestick patterns, and price action to plan my trades.

I have also noticed that market sentiment works better with stocks than indices. This is because indices are more sensitive to global changes, whereas stocks involve limited participation from the people (compared to indices) and align well with market sentiment.

3

Market Open Always Gives a Clue for the Open-Minded Trader

The market doesn't move in a straight line. Even a strong stock goes up, consolidates for some time, and then goes up again. A minor correction is always a sign of a healthy trend, and a rapid price increase without any correction is indicative of something fishy.

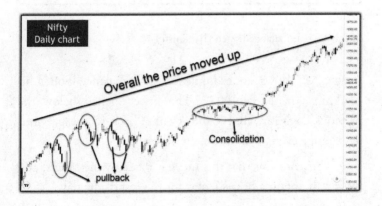

Image 3.1 – Price movement in a daily chart (Nifty)

Image 3.1 shows the Nifty daily chart from Jan 2021 to Oct 2021. Overall, the price moved upside from 13,500 to 18,000. But it witnessed many minor corrections and consolidations before going up.

If we dig deeper, the price gives a clue about the rest of the day's price movement during open itself. It displays an imbalanced open on most trending days, and on most range-bound days, it shows a balanced open.

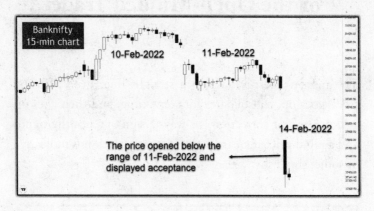

Image 3.2 – Imbalanced open (Banknifty)

Image 3.2 shows an example of an imbalanced open in Banknifty on 14-Feb-2022. The price opened below the previous day's low, and it didn't come back to the previous day's range even 30 minutes after the open.

This confirms that this move is made by big sellers, and we can maintain a bearish view for the rest of the day.

Pro Tip: Options buying works well in these cases, but you should know how to time your entry and exit.

What is a Balanced Open?

In a balanced open, the price opens within the previous day's range, shows acceptance at the center of the last day's range, and doesn't show any signs of breaking the previous day's peaks (high or low) during the first 15-30 minutes of the price action.

If the price opens within the previous day's range and if it is accepted, then the probability of a sideways move within the range of the previous day is very high on that day. This condition is called a balanced market.

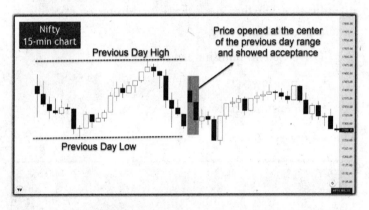

Image 3.3 – Balanced open (Nifty)

Image 3.3 shows an example of a balanced open in Nifty on 17-Feb-2022. The price opened close to the middle part of the previous day's range, and it didn't break either the previous day's low or the previous day's high even after 30 minutes following the open.

This confirms that big players are missing from the game, and we can expect a sideways move within the previous day's range for the rest of the day (unless strong fundamental news comes out in the live market).

Pro Tip: Options-selling strategies such as short straddles or short strangles work well in these cases, but you should have a proper stop-loss plan for their positions in order to avoid unlimited risk while selling options.

Bullish Open Types

Along with the open reference level, the first 15 minutes (after the open) of the price action also plays a crucial role in indicating whether the price is accepting or rejecting at certain price levels.

There are two bullish open types:

- Open-low
- Open-test-drive-up

Open-Low

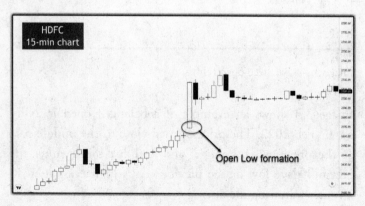

Image 3.4 – An open-low formation (HDFC)

In Image 3.4, the price opened precisely at the previous day's high, and the open-low indicates the swift entry of big buyers. Their strong driving intent

pushed the price on the upside, and the price didn't come back to the open level.

Hence, the open-low formation in the 15-min chart is bullish in nature.

Open-Test-Drive-Up

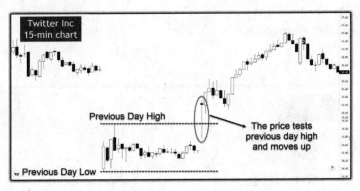

Image 3.5 – An open-test-drive-up formation (Twitter)

This is similar to open-low, but it lacks the initial confidence required to drive the prices immediately after the opening.

The price opens and tests a particular known reference point (resistance or the previous day's high) to ensure that no energy is left in that direction. Then it rallies in the opposite direction.

In Image 3.4, the price opened with a gap above the previous day's range. It came back to test the previous day's high, but some strong buyers absorbed all the selling at open, and hence it closed near the open of the candle (the first candle).

Hence, the open-test-drive-up formation in the 15-minute chart is bullish in nature.

Bearish Open Types

Similar to bullish open types, we have two bearish open types:

- Open-high
- Open-test-drive-down

Open-High

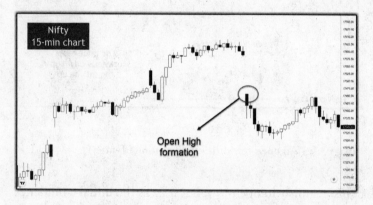

Image 3.6 – An open-high formation (Nifty)

In Image 3.6, the price opened close to the previous day's low, and the open- high indicates the swift entry of strong sellers. Their strong driving intent pushed the price to the downside, and the price didn't come back to the open level.

Hence, the open-high formation in the 15-minute chart is bearish in nature.

Open-Test-Drive-Down

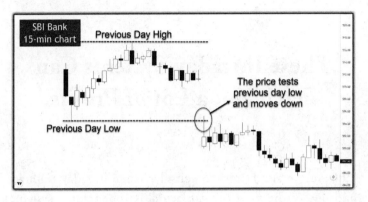

Image 3.7 – An open-test-drive-down formation (SBI Bank)

Open-test-drive-down is similar to open-high, but it lacks the initial confidence required to drive the prices immediately after the open.

The price opens and tests a particular known reference point (support or the previous day's low) to ensure that there is no energy left in that direction, and then it rallies in the opposite direction.

In Image 3.7, the price opened below the previous day's range. It came back to test the previous day's low, but some strong sellers at the open absorbed all the buying, and hence it closes below the previous day's low (the first candle).

Therefore, the open-test-drive-down formation in the 15-minute chart is bearish in nature.

4

These Intraday Systems Can Fetch You a Lot of Profits

There are many factors to consider while intraday trading, and one of the most critical factors is your trading system. A sound trading system will help you make good decisions quickly and efficiently, while a lousy system can lead to costly mistakes.

One of the most significant advantages of using a trading system is that it helps in removing emotions from your trading decisions. While relying on your own judgment, it can be challenging to stay calm and objective when things aren't going your way. A trading system will help you stick to your plan even when the market moves against you.

Another advantage of using a trading system is that it can help you avoid costly mistakes. A bad trade can quickly wipe out your profits or even cause you to lose money. A trading system will allow you to stay focused on your goals and prevent you from making bad trades that can hurt your bottom line.

Intraday System 1 – Buying at Open System (BOS)

This is an excellent system to make an early entry and ride the profits until the end of the day. The only constraint is that traders will have to search for the stocks or indices that satisfy the selection criteria.

Selection Criteria:

Previous day's market sentiment was positive + open-low or open-test-drive-up near the previous day's high in the first 15-minute candle on the current day.

Trade Example 1 – Nifty on 3-Jan-2022

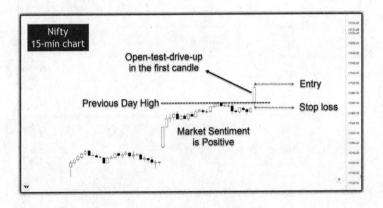

Image 4.1 – BOS trade (Nifty)

Image 4.1 shows an example of a BOS trade opportunity in Nifty.

The market sentiment was positive on the previous day (range shift is positive, range extension is positive, and extreme is neutral). The price showed a perfect open-test-drive-up at the previous day's high level in the first 15-minute candle.

We can plan a long trade above the high of the first candle, keeping a stop- loss below the low of the first candle. It is not good to opt for a fixed target, as these opportunities can go up to more levels. Hence, we can trail SL slowly or keep the stop-loss at entry price once the price moves 1:1 in our direction.

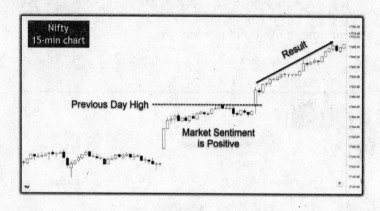

Image 4.2 – BOS trade result (Nifty)

Image 4.2 shows the result of the trade. The entry was triggered in the third candle, and the price closed near the day's high.

We can use this system to trade either stocks or futures instruments (as it is).

Trade Example 2 – Bajaj Finance on 5-Jan-2022

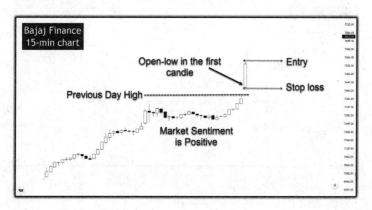

Image 4.3 – BOS trade (Bajaj Finance)

Image 4.3 shows another example of a BOS trade opportunity in Bajaj Finance.

The market sentiment was positive on the previous day (range shift is positive, range extension is positive, and extreme is neutral). The price showed a perfect open-low slightly above the previous day's high level in the first 15-minute candle.

We can plan a long trade above the high of the first candle, keeping a stop- loss below the low of the first candle. We can plan to trail SL slowly or keep the stop-loss at entry price once the price moves 1:1 in our direction.

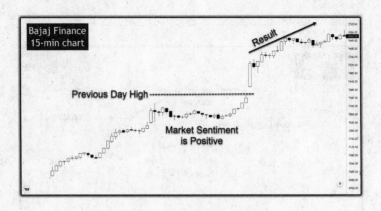

Image 4.4 – BOS trade result (Bajaj Finance)

Image 4.4 shows the result of the trade. The entry was triggered in the second candle, and the price closed near the day's high.

Trade Example 3 – Banknifty on 4-Aug-2021

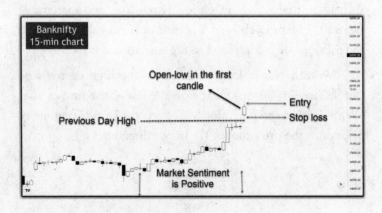

Image 4.5 – BOS trade (Banknifty)

Image 4.5 shows another example of a BOS trade opportunity in Banknifty.

The market sentiment was positive on the previous day (range shift is positive, range extension is positive, and extreme is neutral), and the price showed a similar to open-low (there is a small wick, which is acceptable) slightly above the previous day's high level in the first 15-minute candle.

We can plan a long trade above the high of the first candle, keeping a stop- loss below the low of the first candle. As usual, we can plan to trail SL slowly or keep the stop-loss at entry price once the price moves 1:1 in our direction.

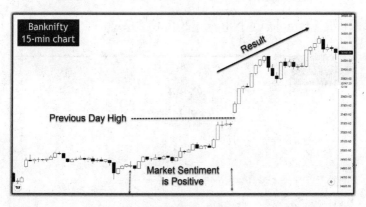

Image 4.6 – BOS trade result (Banknifty)

Image 4.6 shows the result of the trade. The entry was triggered in the second candle, and the price displayed a good move on the upside.

Intraday System 2 – Selling at Open System (SOS)

Like BOS, this is also a good system to make an early entry and ride the profits till the end of the day in a short trade. The only constraint is that traders will have to search for the stocks or indices which satisfy the selection criteria.

Selection Criteria:

Previous day's market sentiment was negative + open-high or open-test-drive- down near the previous day's low in the first 15-minute candle on the current day.

Trade Example 1 – Nifty on 20-July-2021

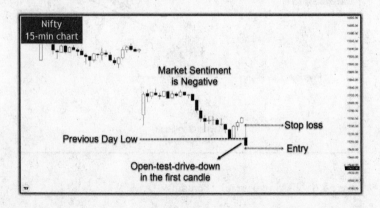

Image 4.7 – SOS trade (Nifty)

Image 4.7 shows an example of an SOS trade opportunity in Nifty.

The market sentiment was negative on the previous day (range shift is negative, range extension is negative, and extreme is neutral). The price showed an open-test-drive-down precisely at the previous day's low level in the first 15-minute candle.

Hence, we can plan a short trade below the first candle's low, keeping a stop- loss above the high of the first candle. As usual, we can plan to trail SL slowly

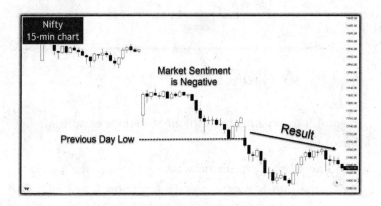

Image 4.8 – SOS trade result (Nifty)

Image 4.8 shows the result of the trade. The entry was triggered in the second candle, and the price displayed a good move on the downside.

Trade Example 2 – Banknifty on 11-Nov-2021

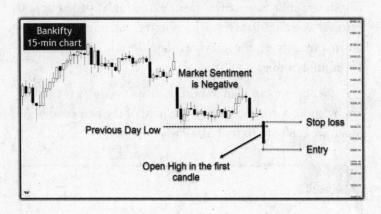

Image 4.9 – SOS trade (Banknifty)

Image 4.9 shows an example of an SOS trade opportunity in Banknifty.

The market sentiment was negative on the previous day (range shift is negative, range extension is neutral, and extreme is neutral). The price showed an open-high precisely at the previous day's low level in the first 15-minute candle. Besides, this level also coincides with the previous swing low.

Hence, we can plan a short trade below the first candle's low, keeping a stop-loss above the high of the first candle. As usual, we can plan to trail SL slowly.

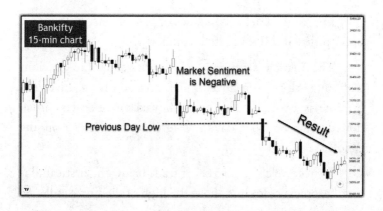

Image 4.10 – SOS trade result (Banknifty)

Image 4.10 shows the result of the trade. The entry was triggered in the fourth candle, and the price displayed a good move on the downside.

Trade Example 3 – HDFC Life Insurance on 07-Feb-2022

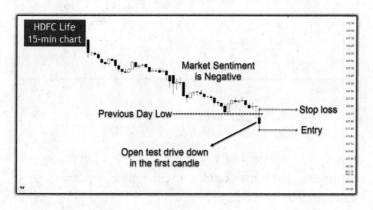

Image 4.11 – SOS trade (HDFC Life Insurance)

Image 4.11 shows an example of an SOS trade opportunity in HDFC Life Insurance.

The market sentiment was negative on the previous day (range shift is negative, range extension is negative, and extreme is neutral). The price showed an open-test-drive-down at the previous day's low level in the first 15-minute candle.

Hence, we can plan a short trade below the first candle's low, keeping a stop- loss above the high of the first candle. As usual, we can plan to trail SL slowly.

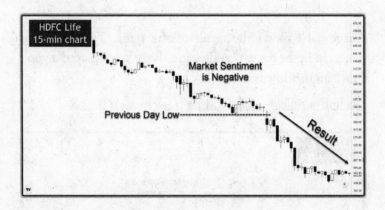

Image 4.12 – SOS trade result (HDFC Life Insurance)

Image 4.12 shows the result of the trade. The entry was triggered in the fourth candle, and the price displayed a good move on the downside.

Precautions To Follow While Using BOS and SOS Systems

Before you decide to use a trading system for stock market trading, it is essential you understand the risks and take the necessary precautions to minimize them.

One of the most significant risks associated with trading systems is emotional trading. When you are trading based on a system, it is essential to be dispassionate and emotionless; otherwise, you may be tempted to override the method or abandon it altogether due to losses.

Another risk is overconfidence. You won't be successful every time just because you have a trading system. There is always the possibility of losses, so it is essential to be realistic about your expectations and follow money management rules accordingly.

It is also important to remember that trading systems are not guaranteed to make money. Even the best strategy can fail, so it is vital to have a solid backup plan in place when it comes to losses.

Overall, trading systems can be a great way to improve your trading results, but it is crucial to understand the risks involved and take appropriate precautions. By doing so, you can minimize your losses and maximize your profits.

Here are some precautions to take before using BOS and SOS trading systems:

➢ Please backtest both BOS and SOS strategies with a minimum of 100 charts. It will clear any confusion in your mind and give you conviction in the system.

➢ Don't add any other technical concepts to them. Always remember that simple is powerful.

➢ You need to wait for the completion of the first candle (15-minute) and avoid taking early entries.

➢ If there is a big gap open or the first candle displays a very big move, avoid the trade.

➢ Intentionally, I have excluded the 'exit' part in both systems. Because every individual is different, one person may hold the trade until the end of the day, whereas another person may prefer to exit the trade in 1 hour. It is your responsibility to find the best exit technique that works for you. Trail SL gives the best results, judging from both my experience as well as backtesting.

Intraday System 3 – Open Range Breakout System (ORBS)

ORB is an intraday trading strategy developed by Toby Crabel. It is one of the most popular strategies among traders.

The first hour after the market opens up is crucial in setting the foundation for anything else that you want to do that day with stocks or futures contracts – which includes overnight trades as well!

There are many variations on this pattern. Some people use 30 minutes, while others prefer 60+6=76 minutes, and so on. But to keep it simple, we will stick to the first 60 minutes as the opening range.

With the ORB strategy, traders wait for 1 hour after the market opens and mark the high and low of the 1-hour range. If the price breaks the high of the 1-hour range, they will opt for a long trade, keeping a stop-loss slightly below the low of the breakout candle.

Similarly, if the price breaks the low of the 1-hour range, they will opt for a short trade, keeping a stop-loss slightly above the high breakdown candle.

However, there is a minor flaw with this system, and if we use it as it is, we may encounter more failed trades. A small fine-tune can help us avoid these failures and generate better results.

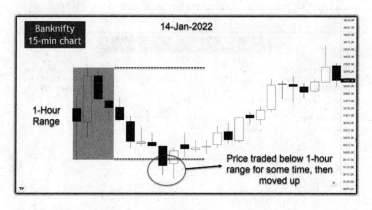

Image 4.13 – ORB failure (short trade)

In Image 4.13, the price traded below the 1-hour range for some time. If a trader opts for a short trade, then the price will hit his stop-loss.

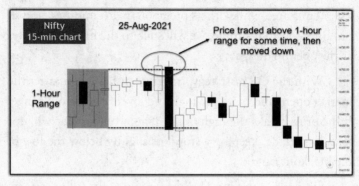

Image 4.14 – ORB failure (long trade)

In Image 4.14, the price traded above the 1-hour range for some time. If a trader opts for a long trade, then the price will hit his stop-loss in the next candle itself.

Hence, I suggest using the filter below, which helps in picking the most successful trades and avoiding failures.

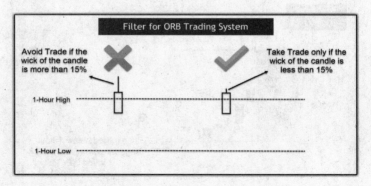

Image 4.15 – Filter for the ORB system in a 15-minute timeframe

Always use the 15-minute timeframe chart to apply this rule. When the 'wick' of the breakout candle (which breaks the 1-hour high) is more than 15% of the entire body, then it is better to avoid the long trade, as there is a high probability of a false breakout.

For example, if the high of the breakout candle is 35,100 and the low is 35,000, then the closure of the candle should be above 35,085 (for 15% of the wick) to opt for a long trade.

The same rules apply for breakdown candles to take short trades. Selection Criteria for Long Trades:

Previous day's market sentiment was positive + breakout candle that breaks the 1-hour high should have less than 15% wick.

Selection Criteria for Short Trades:

Previous day's market sentiment was negative + breakdown candle that breaks the 1-hour low should have less than 15% wick.

<u>Trade Example 1 – Nifty on 28-Feb-2022</u>

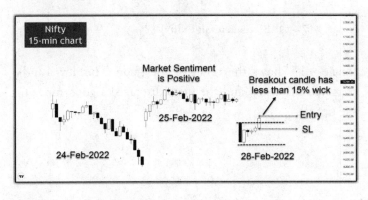

Image 4.16 – ORBS trade (Nifty)

Image 4.16 shows an example of an ORBS trade opportunity in Nifty.

The market sentiment was positive on the previous day (range shift is positive, range extension is positive, and extreme is positive), and the breakout candle contains less than 15% wick.

Hence, we can plan a long trade above the high of the breakout candle, keeping a stop-loss below the low of the same candle. As usual, we can plan to trail SL slowly.

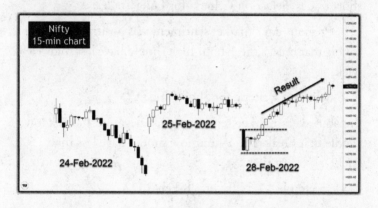

Image 4.17 – ORBS trade result (Nifty)

Image 4.17 shows the result of the trade. The next candle triggered the entry, and the price displayed a good move on the upside.

Trade Example 2 – Banknifty on 27-Jan-2022

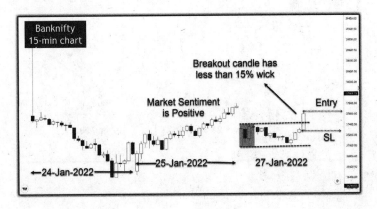

Image 4.18 – ORBS Trade (Banknifty)

Image 4.18 shows an example of an ORBS trade opportunity in Banknifty.

The market sentiment was positive on the previous day (range shift is neutral, range extension is positive, and extreme is neutral), and the breakout candle contains less than 15% wick.

Therefore, we can plan a long trade above the high of the breakout candle, keeping a stop-loss below the low of the same candle. As usual, we can plan to trail SL slowly.

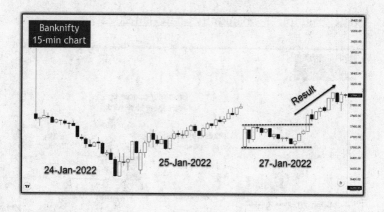

Image 4.19 – ORBS trade result (Banknifty)

Image 4.19 shows the result of the trade. The next candle triggered the entry, and the price displayed a good move on the upside.

Trade Example 3 – Hero MotoCorp on 26-Nov-2021

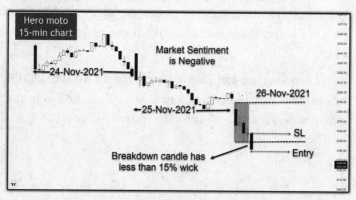

Image 4.20 – ORBS trade (Hero MotoCorp)

Image 4.20 shows an example of an ORBS trade opportunity in Hero MotoCorp.

The market sentiment was negative on the previous day (range shift is negative, range extension is negative, and extreme is neutral), and the breakdown candle contains less than 15% wick.

Hence, we can plan a short trade below the low of the breakdown candle, keeping a stop-loss above the high of the same candle. As usual, we can plan to trail SL slowly.

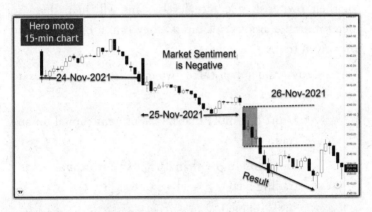

Image 4.21 – ORBS trade result (Hero MotoCorp)

Image 4.21 shows the result of the trade. The next candle triggered the entry, and the price displayed a good move on the downside.

Importance of Money Management

Money management is one of the most important aspects of stock market trading. A well-executed money management plan can help traders stay in the market for the long haul, allowing them to maximize their profits. Without a sound money management plan, traders may quickly lose their capital.

There are a few critical components to a successful money management plan. The first one is to set realistic trading goals and limits. Traders should never risk more money than they can actually afford to lose on any given trade.

Additionally, traders should have a solid understanding of their own risk tolerance levels. This will help them to determine the amount of capital they can afford to risk on any given trade.

Always remember these two rules when it comes to intraday trading:

1. Don't risk more than 2-3% of your capital on any trade.

2. Don't lose more than 10% of your capital on any trading day.

These two rules will help any day trader stay in the market.

Section 3

Options Trading

1

Why Trade in Options?

Before I explain how to take the trade with options for breakout trades, I need to explain some things about options. Most beginners assume options trading is about buying call options (CE) or put options (PE) when they are expecting a good move. But trust me – there's more to options trading than that. We can make money with options when we expect a good move, but we can also make money when we are not expecting one! So please read all the content related to options carefully.

We have three primary trading instruments in the stock market:

1) Equity
2) Futures
3) Options

Equity offers low risk and low reward. Futures offer medium risk and medium reward.

But options are a versatile trading instrument that offers low to significant risk and reward, depending on how the trader uses them.

Besides, it can also be used to protect the portfolio (hedging) and maximize the returns of the portfolio (covered calls). In addition to that, one can calculate how much they earn or lose once the deadline (expiry) arrives.

Both equity and futures are bi-directional products – it means a trader can make money by predicting the direction (either upside or downside). However, a trader can make money irrespective of the direction (up, down, or sideways) with options.

The opposite of 'hedging' is 'speculation,' and the options can also be used for speculation. In addition, options offers the highest risk/reward ratio in the case of speculation compared to both equity and futures.

It offers the following advantages:

1) It has the potential to give higher returns.

2) It can be deployed with a small capital.

3) It provides different varieties of alternative strategies.

2

What is an Option?

An option is a contract that gives a person the right to BUY or SELL an underlying stock/index at a specific price (known as the 'strike price') within a deadline (known as the 'expiry').

Let's say that you are buying a contract to buy XYZ shares at 100 by the end of the month. Here, you are not obligated to buy XYZ shares at 100, but you retain the right (to buy) till the end of the month, which is why it's called an 'option' rather than a 'mandatory.'

However, this right comes with a small fee, called a 'premium'. There are two types of contracts:

1) **Call Options** (**CE**) – Allows for buying a stock at a specified price within the expiry.

2) **Put Options** (**PE**) – Allows for selling a stock at a specified price within the expiry.

Let me give a real-life example to help you better understand these options.

Many people have the dream of one day owning a house. Let's say that you have finalized a flat with a reputed builder in an excellent residential area.

The builder will be delivering the flat 2 years from now, and he is quoting ₹50,00,000 for the flat.

With the current setup, a person is going to buy this flat by paying ₹50,00,000 in advance (or in installments).

But what will happen if the builder doesn't complete the project within 2 years?

In addition, you are at risk if someone files a legal case against the entire project. Do you agree?

These are small elements of the risk, and you don't want to lose the flat because a metro project is being undertaken nearby, and there is a high probability that the cost of the apartment will double in value.

What if a builder comes up with a contract saying that you will retain the right to buy the flat for ₹50,00,000 at any time within the next 2 years, but that you don't own the flat in this contract period and you need to pay ₹50,000 to own these rights?

You would gladly accept it, right? By spending just ₹50,000, you would retain the right to buy the flat at ₹50,00,000 for the next 2 years.

Moreover, you don't own the flat, and in case any issues arise, you can always opt out of buying the flat and would only lose ₹50,000 if you did.

But if there were no issues, and the metro project goes through, then the price of the flat would go up. For the sake of explanation, assume that the new price is ₹90,00,000, and you have the right to buy it for ₹50,00,000.

What would you do?

You would surely buy it, right?

Let's go one step deeper.

Assume that you don't have ₹50,00,000 in capital to buy the flat at the end of the 2 years. What would your plan of action be in this case?

You could plan to sell the contract to another person (because they could buy the flat for ₹50,00,000, whereas the current price is ₹90,00,000).

Now, would you sell the contract for just ₹50,000? I'm sure you wouldn't.

You would sell it for a higher price, and the other person (who is buying the rights) would also be happy to buy it at this higher price because he would save ₹40,00,000 (as he gets the right to buy the flat at ₹50,00,000).

Even if you sell the contract for ₹5,00,000, you would have made a 10x profit on your original capital.

If we look at the above example in terms of options trading, then it would look like this:

Options Type – Call Options (CE)

Strike Price – ₹50,00,000

Expiry – 2 years

Premium – ₹50,000

This is what happens with options trading.

Most of us don't buy/sell the underlying stocks (except for a few hedge funds and institutions). We buy/sell the rights (options contracts) to make money in the market.

3

Options Trading Jargon

By now, you know most of the terms related to options trading. However, it is better to understand all the terms associated with options.

Option Premium

The price that the buyer of the option gives to the option seller/writer.

Strike Price

The price at which the option buyer and option seller make the contract. It is also called the 'exercised price.'

For example, Banknifty is trading at 33265. A trader thinks it will go above 34200 in a week, so he will buy 34200 CE, assuming he will make money. Here, 34200 is one strike price.

Similarly, security will have different strike prices to facilitate the trade between option buyers and option sellers.

Expiry Date

The last date specified in the option contract. It is also called an exercise date.

After the expiry date, options traders cannot exercise their options.

American Option

A type of option that can be exercised on any date before the expiry.

European Option

A type of option that can be exercised only on the expiry day. All the options instruments in India support only European options (hence the name CE and PE).

4

Long vs. Short in Options Trading

When a trader buys some shares of a stock anticipating that the price will go up in the future, it is called a 'long' position.

In contrast, it is called a 'short' position when a trader first sells some shares of the stock (without having any position in the same stock) anticipating that the price will fall in the future.

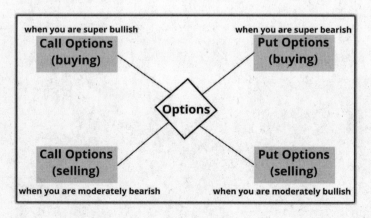

Image 4.1 – Options trading methods

But unlike stocks, if a trader buys CE (anticipating the price will go up) or PE (anticipating the price will go down), it is recognized as a 'long' position in options (option buyer).

If a trader sells CE (anticipating the price will go down) or PE (anticipating the price will go up), it is recognized as a 'short' position in options (option seller or option writer).

Long call – for a bullish view

Long put – for a bearish view

Short call – for a bearish view

Short put – for a bullish view

5

ITM, ATM, and OTM in Options Trading

What is an In-The-Money (ITM) Option?

An ITM option results in positive cash flow in favor of the holder if it is exercised immediately.

For CE – when the spot price is higher than the strike price.

For PE – when the spot price is lower than the strike price.

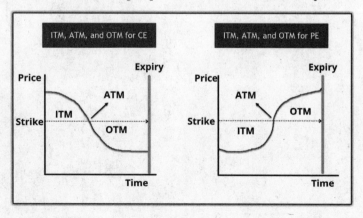

Image 5.1 – ITM, ATM, and OTM in options trading

What is an At-The-Money (ATM) Option?

An ATM option results in zero cash flow to the holder if it is exercised immediately.

For CE – when the spot price is equal to the strike price.
For PE – when the spot price is equal to the strike price.

What is an Out-The-Money (OTM) Option?

An OTM option results in negative cash flow to the holder if exercised immediately.

For CE – when the spot price is lower than the strike price.

For PE – when the spot price is higher than the strike price.

6

Greeks in Options

Option Greeks are various parameters that affect the premium in real-time.

Therefore, it will benefit an options trader to keep an eye on these parameters to reap the maximum benefits and avoid significant losses with options trading.

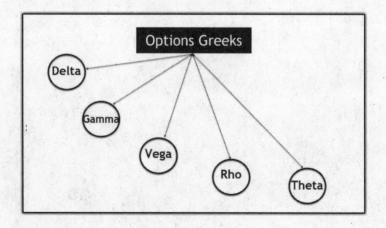

Image 6.1 – Options Greeks

Delta

It measures the rate of change of option premium concerning change in the underlying price.

Gamma

It is the change in option Delta per unit change in the stock price. In simple terms, it measures the rate of change of Delta.

If the Gamma is high, the Delta will be highly sensitive to option prices. Among OTM, ITM, and ATM options, ATM options will have the highest gamma.

Theta

It measures the impact on the option premium concerning the time remaining for expiry.

Vega

It is the rate of change in the premium concerning change in the volatility. If the option Vega is high (either positive or negative), the option premium values are highly sensitive to any changes in the volatility.

Rho

It measures the rate of change concerning interest rate.

7

How to Trade Options

I will give a simple example to help you understand how individuals' perspectives give different results while trading options.

Please note that the trading idea mentioned below is an example of different results around options buying and options selling.

Scrip – HDFC Bank
Date – 17-May-2021
Expiry – 27-May-2021
Strike Price – 1500
Qty Per Lot – 550

Case 1 – John as an Option Buyer

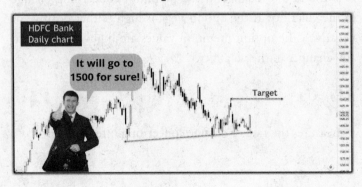

Image 7.1 – An options buying trade (HDFC)

Image 7.1 shows a daily chart for HDFC Bank. The price is taking the support 1360-1380 levels.

Besides, HDFC Bank belongs to the top 10 stocks in Nifty.

Thus, John, who is a trader, thinks that the price will go up from here. Besides, he also predicts that it can go up to 1500 levels, which is the immediate resistance.

Call Option May 1500 is trading at 5.35.

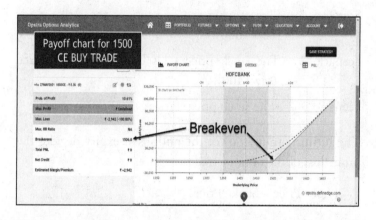

Image 7.2 – Payoff chart for options buying

In any trade, three parameters are essential:

1) Success probability

2) Maximum risk

3) Maximum reward.

If you look at the payout chart of the 1500 CE buy trade (Image 7.2), the probability of success is only 10.61%, the maximum risk is only ₹2,942 (also the required capital), and the maximum reward is unlimited. The profit depends on where the price will close above 1506 (1500 + premium paid).

In simple terms, there is a 10.61% probability of making unlimited profits, or an 89.39% probability of losing ₹2,942 in an attempt to make some profits.

The expiry is around 10 days away, and broadly speaking, there are three possible scenarios:

Scenario 1 – The stock price goes above the strike price (say 1600).

Scenario 2 – The stock price stays below the strike price (say 1400).

Scenario 3 – The stock price stays at 1500.

The intrinsic value (IV) of the options at expiry decides the profit/loss of the options trade.

IV = Spot Price – Strike Price

We need to include the premium paid (₹5.35/-) in our calculation.

Profit/Loss in Scenario 1

1600 (spot) – 1500 (strike) = 100
Subtract the premium paid, 100-5.35 = 94.65
The profit is ₹94.65.

Total profit per lot (550 QTY) = ₹94.65 x 550 = ₹52,057

Profit/Loss in Scenario 2

1400 (spot) – 1500 (strike) = -100
But IV should be a non-negative number; hence, we leave it to zero. There is no need to exercise this option.
Therefore, the loss is ₹5.35 (premium paid).

Total loss per lot (550 QTY) = ₹5.35 x 550 = ₹2942.5

Profit/Loss in Scenario 3

1500 (spot) – 1500 (strike) = 0
Subtract the premium paid, 0-5.35 = -5.35
Hence, the loss is ₹5.35 (premium paid).

Total loss per lot (550 QTY) = ₹5.35 x 550 = ₹2942.5

Case 2 – Sheela as an Option Seller

Image 7.3 – Options selling trade

Sheela is an expert options trader, and she thinks that the price will not reach 1500 within the expiry (the next 10 days), because of the overall negative market sentiment.

Hence, she decides to sell the same option 1500 CE (or the opposite side of John). After executing the trade, she immediately gets the premium of ₹5.35 in her account.

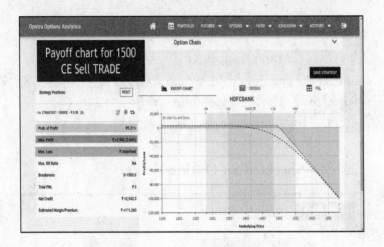

Image 7.4 – Payoff chart for options selling

If you look at the payout chart of the 1500 CE sell trade (Image 7.4), the probability of success is 89.21%, the maximum risk is unlimited, and the ultimate reward is only ₹2,942. But the capital required to execute this trade is ₹1,11,260 (due to exchange rules).

Profit depends on where the price will close below 1505 (1500 + premium received).

In simple terms, there is an 89.21% probability of making a profit of ₹2,942, or a 10.89% probability of losing an unlimited sum in an attempt to make some profits (unlimited losses can be avoided by closing the trade or by hedging).

The expiry is around 10 days away, and we consider the same three possible scenarios from the last example:

Scenario 1 – The stock price goes above the strike price (say 1600). Scenario 2 – The stock price stays below the strike price (say 1400). Scenario 3 – The stock price stays at 1500.

The intrinsic value (IV) of the options at the expiry decides the profit/loss of the options trade.

IV = Spot Price – Strike Price

We need to include the premium paid (₹5.35/-) in our calculation.

Profit/Loss in Scenario 1

1600 (spot) – 1500 (strike) = 100
Subtract the premium paid, 100-5.35 = 94.65
So the loss is ₹94.65.

Total loss per lot (550 QTY) = ₹94.65 x 550 = ₹52,057

Profit/Loss in Scenario 2

1400 (spot) – 1500 (strike) = Spot is less than the strike price. Hence the profit is the entire premium received.

The profit is ₹5.35 (premium received).

Total profit per lot (550 QTY) = ₹5.35 x 550 = ₹2,942

Profit/Loss in Scenario 3

1500 (spot) – 1500 (strike) = 0

Hence, the profit is ₹5.35 (premium received).

Total profit per lot (550 QTY) = ₹5.35 x 550 = ₹2,942

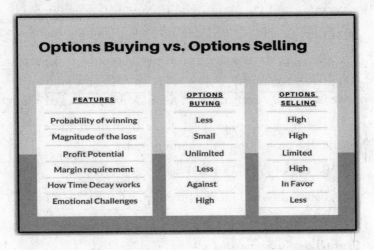

Image 7.5 – Options buying vs. options selling

Both options buying and option selling have their own advantages and disadvantages.

It is essential to understand all these features before attempting to take options trades.

Please note that these disadvantages can be negated with slight adjustments and countertrades.

For example, if a trader has a simple thumb rule of exiting his options selling position if the price reaches the strike price, then he has removed the maximum loss scenario from his trading (except for massive gap scenarios).

8

Role of Time Decay in Options Trading

Before exploring different options trading strategies or trade in options, it is crucial to understand how the significant factors affect the option premium.

As you know, underlying instrument prices (Delta and Gamma) majorly impact the option premium. The direction and magnitude of the underlying instruments can be predicted using technical analysis.

Apart from Delta and Gamma, the next important factor which affects the option premium is time decay (Theta).

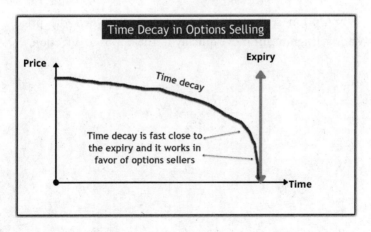

Image 8.1 – Time decay in options

As shown in Image 8.1, time decay favors option sellers. It will be aggressive when the option contract is close to the expiry. All OTM options quickly run toward zero at the time of expiry, and many option sellers attempt to make some profits from this move.

Because of this reason, option selling provides the highest winning probability compared to option buying.

For example, let's say a trader analyzes a stock and concludes that it will go up in the next few days, so he decides to sell put options to get the premium in his pockets.

He will only lose money if the price starts to trade below his options strike price. In all other cases, i.e. when the price is upside down or goes sideways, he will make money.

However, option selling can also bring unlimited losses (or huge losses) if the price moves in the opposite direction. A trader can mitigate this risk in two ways: 1) placing an SL buy order, and 2) hedging.

Option sellers will lose money only when the price shows a significant move quickly in the opposite direction.

9

Importance of Strike Price in Options Trading

The strike price is the fixed price at which the underlying instrument (stock or index) can be bought or sold.

When a trader buys a call option, he is purchasing the right to buy the stock/index at a predetermined price.

Let's say that you have decided to sell the same call option at the same strike price and expiry.

It indicates that you are selling the buyer the right to purchase the stock at a predetermined price (the strike price), and hence you receive a premium.

The strike price also plays a crucial role. Don't forget that if the underlying instrument doesn't reach the strike price, then the premium becomes zero. But if you select a very far strike price, you will receive a low premium, which reduces the ROI for your trade.

Let's look at an example.

Date: 18th May 2021, Time: 10:00 a.m. (IST)

Instrument – Nifty

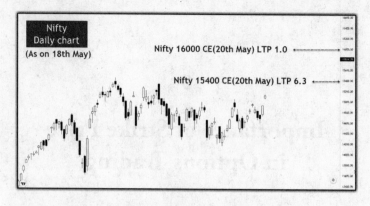

Image 9.1 – Importance of strike price in options trading

Let's say that an option seller develops a bearish view (for whatever reason) and decides to sell the call option.

There are 3 trading days remaining (including 18th May, as the time is 10 a.m.) for the expiry.

If he sells 15400 CE, he will get a premium of 6.3, and if he sells 16000 CE, he will receive a premium of 1.0.

So, if he opts for 15400 CE at 6.3, then the ROI for the trade will be good, but there is a higher probability of the price closing above 15400.

If he opts for 16000 CE, the ROI is less, but there is a very high probability that the price will not close above 16000.

So, a trader has to balance these two aspects in his trading.

In the above example, if the trader opts for 15500 or 15600 CE, he can still make a decent ROI (compared to 16000 CE) for his trade with increased probability (compared to 15400 CE).

10

Options Trading – Buying or Selling?

Options buying is the process of buying an option contract with the anticipation that the underlying security will rise in price (buying CE) or anticipation that the underlying security's price will fall (buying PE).

Options selling, also known as writing options, is the process of selling an option contract with the anticipation that the underlying asset will fall in price (selling CE) or that the underlying asset price will rise (selling PE).

Options buying or options selling – which is better? The answer to this question depends on several factors, including your risk tolerance, your trading goals, the market conditions, and your personality traits.

At first sight, options buying looks like a more conservative strategy than options selling because when you buy an option, you are only risking the premium you paid for the contract. If the underlying asset does not move in the direction you predicted, you can simply let the option expire and lose only the premium.

But the failure rate is always high with options buying, which can demotivate the trader and encourage them to take a higher risk on the next trade or make them fall into the trap of revenge trading.

On the other hand, when you sell an option, you risk your entire capital. If the underlying asset moves in the wrong direction, you could lose a lot of money (if there is no hedging or exit plan). Therefore, options selling is generally considered a riskier strategy than options buying.

There are times when options selling can be more profitable than options buying because it offers a higher success rate compared to options buying, as the time decay (theta) works in favor of the options sellers.

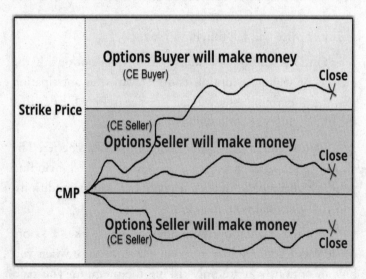

Image 10.1 – Options buying vs. options selling

As shown in Image 10.1, a call option (CE) buyer will make money only when the price closes above his strike price. In all other cases (when price moves downside or when price moves sideways), he will lose money.

However, a call options (CE) seller will make money if the price closes below the strike price (in case of either a sideways or downside move). So, the option seller has a high probability of success, but his profits are always limited.

A trader should do some introspection before opting for options buying or options selling. If they can digest more failures but are keen to make big money when they are right, they can go with options buying. Otherwise, if a trader is prone to experiencing emotional distress when their trades fail, it is better to stick with selling options.

We need to take a keen look at the price action as well. When we expect a big move in the next few candles, buying options makes sense. Otherwise, if we expect a slow move, it is better to stick to selling options.

We can use options buying for Buying at Open System (BOS) and Selling at Open Systems (SOS), but one should develop a proper exit plan (either partial exit or trail SL) based on their personality.

We can deploy options selling for Open Range Breakout Systems (ORBS), as these moves often come with slow moves.

Section 4

Trading for Beginners

1

Why Everyone Should Know About Stock Markets

One can buy and sell stocks in the stock market, which represent shares in listed businesses. The stock market is a collection of markets where listed stocks/companies are traded. You're participating in the stock market whenever you buy or sell stocks.

The stock market is essential because businesses raise money through stock markets to grow. Companies use the funds they raise from selling stocks to expand their businesses, hire new employees, and make other investments.

When you invest in a stock, you're hoping that the stock you've bought will increase in value over time. This increase in value is called capital gain. You can make money from capital gains by selling your stocks for more than you paid (the buy price) for them.

Inflation is when the cost of goods and services increases over time. It is difficult to beat inflation with fixed deposits (FD) in banks, as they offer lower interest rates. It is possible to beat inflation with real estate investments, but they always demand high capital and often come with legal risks.

Hence, the stock market is a great way to beat inflation. When you invest in the stock market, your money will grow at a higher rate than the rate of inflation. This means that your money will be worth more in the future.

When you invest/trade in the stock market, you're taking on some risk, but you're also learning about how investments/trades work. If you lose money in the stock market, you'll learn from your mistakes and become a better investor.

The stock market is a great way to make money (if you make the right decisions), but it's also a great way to lose money (if you make wrong decisions). So before you trade/invest in the stock market, make sure you understand the risks involved.

2

Some Basic Concepts You Must Know About the Stock Market

Different countries have different business structures for companies. Some well-known structures are sole proprietorships, partnerships, private limited companies, and public limited companies. All these business structures can be classified broadly as either **public** or **private** companies.

Except for sole proprietorships, most companies have many shareholders. A shareholder is a person who holds one or many shares of the company, and hence they are the partial owner of the company.

So when you purchase a share of Reliance or Tesla stock, you are actually buying a small ownership stake in the company. This also provides voting rights in some issues, allows you to collect the dividends after AGMs, and lets you participate in the growth/fall of the company in the future.

Stock Exchange

A stock exchange is a common platform that connects the buyers and sellers in the market.

A company has to first list on the exchanges before people can buy and sell its shares. The National Stock Exchange (NSE) and the Bombay Stock Exchange (BSE) are the popular stock exchanges in India. Similarly, NASDAQ and NYSE are the popular stock exchanges in the US. There is also the Singapore Exchange (SGX), a famous stock exchange in Singapore, the Stock Exchange of Thailand (SET), the ASX and NSX in Australia, and so on.

Every exchange comes with its own criteria for listing companies. There is also the possibility of buying and selling shares of some companies through the over-the-counter (OTC) method, but it comes with its own risks, and most beginners should only focus on buying/selling stocks from the popular exchanges.

Index

A stock exchange is a marketplace where shares of many companies can be bought and sold. Whereas an index is a list of selected stocks from the exchange to indicate how well the markets are performing in a broader sense.

For example, Nifty is the index of NSE, and it is made up of the top 50 companies from the NSE. Similarly, Sensex is the index of BSE and is made up of the top 30 companies. The S&P 500 is made up of the 500 largest companies, and the Dow Jones is made up of the top 30 companies.

The prices of all the selected underlying stocks in an index are taken into consideration to arrive at the index's overall value.

Traders often take their trades on indices using future or options trading instruments. Investors use these indices to assess the performance of a specific section of the market. For example, do you want to know how IT stocks are doing in India? Look at the CNX IT (or the Nifty IT). Similarly, Banknifty indicates the performance of Indian banks.

Stock Broker

A stock broker acts as a bridge between the stock exchange and people. They provide a platform to receive, buy, and sell information of shares online and over the phone and execute trades on behalf of the people by charging a small commission for the same.

There are two types of brokers: 1) Brokers who execute only your trades, and 2) Brokers who execute your trades and give trading/investment advice.

Initial Public Offer (IPO)

An initial public offering (IPO) is the first time a company offers its shares to the public. When a company goes public, it sells its shares to investors to raise money to grow its business.

An IPO investment can be risky because there is no guarantee that the company's stock price will increase after it goes public. However, there is also the potential for big profits if the stock price rises significantly after the IPO.

There are several things to consider before investing in an IPO, including the company's financial stability, the strength of its management, and the competitive landscape in which it operates. It is also essential to be aware of the risks involved in investing in a newly established public company.

Listing a company for IPO is a lengthy process. Many investors would be excited, as it would be the first time company shares are available to the public. Also, they would be curious to see how the company's share price will perform after the debut.

Bull Market and Bear Market

A bull market is a marketplace where prices rise and investor confidence is high. Bull markets usually appear when the economy is strong and growing. Consumers have more money to spend, so they buy more products and services. This increased demand causes prices to go up.

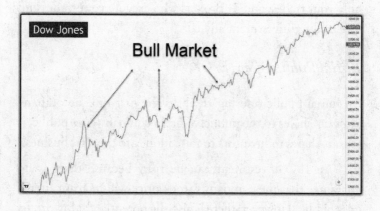

Image 2.1 – A bull market

The businesses that sell these products and services make more money, hiring more workers. This increase in employment causes wages to go up, which causes even more spending by consumers. This positive feedback loop creates a bull market.

On the other hand, a bear market is a market in which prices are falling and investor confidence is low. Bear markets usually appear when the economy is weak or contracting. Consumers have less cash/money to spend, so they buy fewer products and services. This decreased demand causes prices to go down.

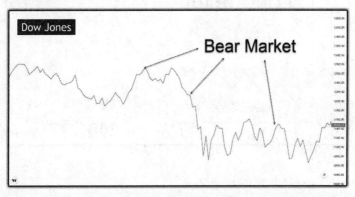

Image 2.2 – A bear market

The businesses that sell these products and services make less money, so they lay off workers. This decrease in employment causes wages to go down, which causes even less spending by consumers. This negative feedback loop creates a bear market.

It's important to remember that not all stocks or markets rise during a bull market. Some stocks may not perform well, while others do well. Similarly, not all stocks or markets fall during a bear market. Some may perform well, while others do poorly. It's also important to remember that bull and bear

markets can last for different lengths of time. A bull market might last for several years, while a bear market might only last for a few months.

Long Trades vs. Short Trades

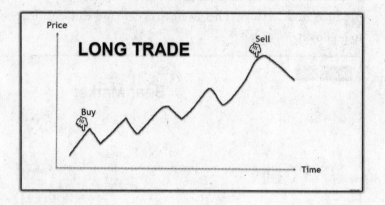

Image 2.3 – A long trade

When a trader anticipates that the price of a stock will go up in the future, he will buy shares of the stock and sell it later when the price goes up. This is called a 'long trade' or a 'long position.' In simple terms, when you open a long position in the market, you are betting that the stock price will increase.

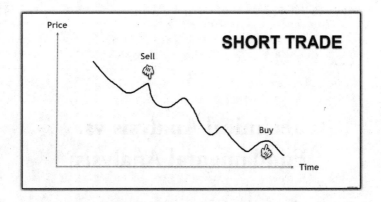

Image 2.4 – A short trade

Taking long trades is a good option when we have a bull market, but in a bear market, long trades will not give profits as the price continuously falls.

Hence, a trader can sell first at a higher price and then buy back later at a lower price to make profits. This is called a 'short trade' or a 'short position'. In simple terms, when you open a short position, you are betting that the stock price will decrease.

The key difference between long and short positions is that when you are long, your potential losses are limited to the amount you paid for the stock (because a stock price can only go to zero in the worst-case scenario).

However, when you are short, your potential losses are unlimited (at least theoretically), as there is no limit to how high the stock can go.

3

Technical Analysis vs. Fundamental Analysis

When analyzing markets, there are two schools of thought. One is fundamental analysis, and the other is technical analysis.

Fundamental analysis looks at factors such as price movements based on supply and demand, the company's financials, and business prospects to predict future trends.

Technical analysis looks at past prices/volume data and suggests that we can use patterns seen in data for accurate insights to try and predict future movements.

Fundamental analysts tend to be more long-term oriented, while technical analysts are more short-term oriented. However, many successful investors use a combination of both fundamental and technical analysis to make investment decisions.

Fundamental Analysis

Fundamental analysis is when you study a company's business to understand its needs. For example, let's say you want to gift some sweets to all of your friends and relatives on a special occasion. What would you do? You would go to the best sweet shop in the market and taste the sweets before buying them. This seems to be the most convenient way to make the purchase.

Let's say you bought the sweets from Kanti Sweets, and everyone liked them. Now you decide to buy the entire Kanti Sweets business. What is your plan of action? Buying Kanti Sweets (the company) will, of course, not be as simple as buying its sweets (the end products), because the capital required to purchase a company is enormous.

Along with capital limitation, as an investor, you should also look at other aspects of the business. This is why we use fundamental analysis. It

helps you identify good companies that are trading at reasonable price levels (below the intrinsic price level).

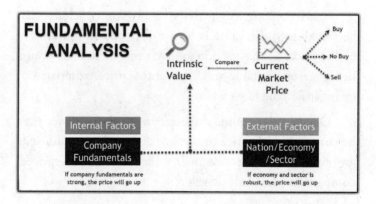

Image 3.1 – Fundamental analysis

Fundamental analysis is a way of figuring out how much a stock is worth. You look at the company's financial statements and how it is doing compared to other companies in that industry. You also consider other aspects, such as the economy and world affairs.

Basically, there are two types of fundamental analysis:

1. **Quantitative** – This analysis is based on numbers, like the company's financial statements (ex. P/E ratio, market cap, quarterly results, cashflow, etc.) and arriving at a share price.

2. Qualitative – **This involves the economy, brand** value, capability of management, etc. and includes these factors when considering the intrinsic value of the stock.

Intrinsic value is the 'fair price' that a typical investor aims to pay for a stock to buy it.

If, after a complete analysis, an investor concludes that the stock's intrinsic value is higher than the stock's current market price, he may decide to invest money into it because the shares are available at a 'discounted' price (compared to the intrinsic value).

On the other hand, if the intrinsic value is lower than the current market price of the stock, then the investor may not buy the shares because their value is already 'overpriced' (compared to the intrinsic value).

Important Parameters in Fundamental Analysis

Investors use many parameters when performing a fundamental analysis to assess a company's financial health. The most famous parameters are inclined toward earnings, growth, and market value.

Here are some of the essential parameters:

Earnings-per-share

EPS is the small portion of the company's profit assigned to each share of its stock. A linear increase in EPS indicates that the share value increases with time, and is a good sign for investors.

EPS = Total Earning / Outstanding Share

Where 'total earning' is nothing but the net profit after tax and other expenses.

'Outstanding share' is the total number of shares owned by the public.

For example, if the company reports a profit of $100 million and there are 50 million shares, then the EPS is $2.0.

Price-to-Earnings (P/E) Ratio

The P/E ratio shows the relationship between stock price and its per share earnings.

P/E Ratio = Stock Price Per Share / Earnings Per Share

The P/E ratio helps people to know whether the stock is overvalued or undervalued compared to other companies in the same sector.

A lower P/E ratio indicates that the current stock price is low compared to its earnings, which is good for investors.

Cash flow

A good business/company should generate sufficient amounts of cash flow every quarter.

There are three types of cash flow: 1) Operating cash flow, 2) Investing cash flow, and 3) Financing cash flow

Among these three, operating cash flow plays a crucial role. A negative operating cash flow indicates that the company is not heading in the right direction.

You can look at any company that experienced bankruptcy; its operating cash flow would have been negative for the last few quarters/years.

Debt-to-Equity (D/E) Ratio

This ratio indicates the relationship between the borrowed capital of the company and the capital provided by its shareholders.

D/E Ratio = Total Liabilities / Total Capital by Shareholders

If a company takes on too much debt, it may go bankrupt if it fails to meet its obligations. For this reason, it is wise for investors to avoid companies with very high levels of debt. To be safe, you should only invest in companies with a D/E ratio of 1 or less.

Let's say you need to shortlist one company among two companies:

1) A, with a D/E ratio of 0.7

2) B, with a D/E ratio of 3.1

In this case, it is better to choose A, as it is less likely to go bankrupt than B. The second company is more likely to go bankrupt due to its high D/E ratio.

Promoters Shareholding

One important criterion for choosing stocks is the promoter's shareholding. The promoter is the person who knows the company best, as they are an insider. They know what is happening in the company and whether it is growing or not.

If the promoter's stake in the company increases, it is a good signal, and we should buy the stock. This means that the promoters are confident about the company's future.

If the promoter's stake in the company decreases, it is a bad signal, and we shouldn't plan to buy it. If we already have this stock in our portfolio, then we should plan to sell it.

Conclusion

All the fundamental analysis indicators are crucial in their own way. These indicators can help you understand how much a stock is worth and how much it can grow. But there are other things as well that affect stock prices, which are harder to measure.

When you're thinking about investing in a company, it's good to use fundamental analysis and other tools like technical analysis, macroeconomic news, and industry-specific data.

Technical Analysis

Technical analysis is the study of past price movements to predict future price movements. People who engage in this use technical concepts and indicators which help them understand what is likely to happen.

The logical theory behind technical analysis is that the collective actions of all the participants in the market accurately reflect all relevant information about a stock. This means that the market always assigns a fair price to security.

Price Discounts Everything

The technical analysis community is widely known for focusing only on price analysis, and they firmly believe that **price discounts all fundamental information.**

Technical analysts believe that there is no need to study the fundamental parameters as all this information is already factored into the price of the stock, thereby making technical analysis more critical.

History Repeats

One of the things that technical analysts believe is that history repeats itself. They believe this because security prices tend to move cyclically over time and because of the human emotions that come into play in the market. If you look at alternating bull markets and bear markets, it makes sense to think about market psychology in a broader sense.

People who do technical analysis often look at chart patterns to see how the market has behaved in the past. They use this information to predict how the market might behave in the future.

Price Moves in Trends

One of the common assumptions made by technical analysis is that prices move in trends, and not randomly.

Most technical analysts believe that prices move in trends of different time periods, like short-term, medium-term, and long-term. This is why they examine data and chart patterns of historical prices and current ones to predict future moves.

These are some of the crucial aspects of technical analysis:

- Chart types
- Price patterns
- Technical indicators
- Candlestick patterns

- Support and resistance
- Types of trading

In the following chapters, we will explore all these aspects one by one.

Conclusion

Technical analysis looks at the price movements and volume of a security. On the other hand, fundamental analysis looks at a company's intrinsic value.

This is determined by the company's financial statements, the overall economy and market conditions, and other liabilities and assets.

There is no one right method to trade stocks, and everyone has their own methods that works for them. So, find what works for you and stick with it! Ultimately, the most important thing is to use the method of analysis that works best for you and to develop your trading style.

4

Types of Charts in Trading

Stock chart patterns are an essential tool for traders. People use them to see how the market is doing. They can use them to look at trends in the market. The price is represented in many chart patterns. Some vital chart types are as follows:

- Line
- Bar
- Candlestick
- Renko
- Point-and-figure
- Heikin-Ashi
- Kagi

The candlestick chart is the most popular and visually appealing chart type among all of them. However, it is good to know about the other chart types that are used.

Line Charts

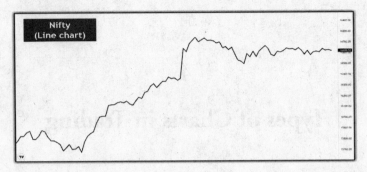

Image 4.1 – A line chart (Nifty)

A line chart is a type of chart that connects the closing prices for each period over the selected timeframe.

It does not contain open, high, or low values of the selected period, unlike a candlestick chart. Investors use this chart to spot trends.

Bar Charts

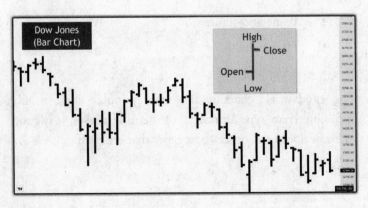

Image 4.2 – A bar chart (Dow Jones)

A bar chart is a graph that has vertical lines that show the price range for a specific period. It also has horizontal dashes on each side showing open and close prices. People also call this type of graph an OHLC chart because it shows the open, high, low, and close.

The opening price is the small horizontal dash on the left, and the small horizontal dash on the right represents the closing price.

In most software, the color of the entire bar is constant. However, in some instances, the bar is green when the closing price is above the open price, and the bar is red when the closing price is below the open price.

Candlestick Charts

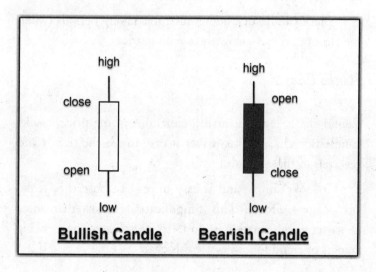

Image 4.3 – A candlestick chart

4.4. A candlestick chart (USD-JPY)

The rising time period (when the closing price is above the opening price) will have hollow bodies.

Black candlestick bodies resemble falling periods (when the closing price is below the opening price).

Renko Charts

Renko charts remove small fluctuations in the price, unlike candlestick charts. This makes it easy to see the trends and reversals in those trends.

It looks simple and is easy to read because the Renko bricks are uniform. This simplification means that some short-term information is lost. In most cases, only swing traders or trend followers use this chart.

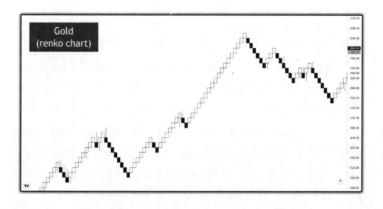

Image 4.5 – A Renko chart (Gold)

The vital step in setting up a Renko chart is to set the size of the brick (which is constant across bricks). It can be 25 points in some stocks, 10-20 pips in the forex market, or some dynamic value based on the average true range (ATR).

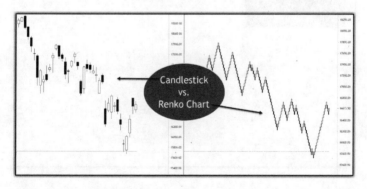

Image 4.6 – A candlestick chart vs. a Renko chart for the same period (Nifty)

The most vital difference between Renko charts and candlestick charts is that Renko charts are smooth.

Image 4.6 shows both the candlestick and Renko chart for Nifty between Jan-2022 till mid-March-2022. The Renko chart displays a smooth price action as it cuts out the noise.

All Renko bricks are of the same length and look identical. A new brick always appears at the top or bottom of the current brick, which means that the price action is only plotted at angles of +45 degrees or -45 degrees.

Point-and-Figure Charts

A point-and-figure chart completely ignores the 'time' parameter while plotting the charts for any trading securities.

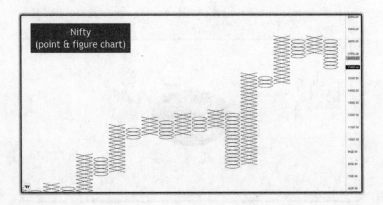

Image 4.7 – A point-and-figure chart (Nifty)

Compared to candlestick charts, point-and-figure charts plot only vertical columns, consisting of X's and O's, depending on the price, which moves upside or downside.

An X indicates a rise in prices, whereas an O suggests a fall. Many traders who study point-and-figure charts say that it is easy to identify where the support and resistance levels lie on them. They also use these charts to identify breakouts and false breakouts.

Heikin-Ashi Charts

Heikin-Ashi charts use data from two time periods to create a candle. They use the 'open-close' information from the prior period candle and the 'open-high-low-close' data from the current period candle to create Heikin-Ashi candlestick.

This makes the chart look smoother and makes it easier to see the trend. Heikin-Ashi candles are good for capturing trends because they remove the gaps between candles and filter out the noise.

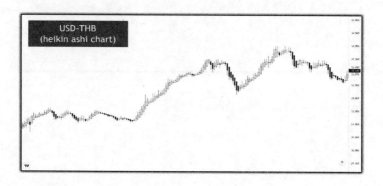

Image 4.8 – A Heikin-Ashi chart (USD-THB)

Here are some interesting features of Heikin-Ashi charts:

- The bullish candles with no lower wick indicate a strong uptrend.

- Small candles with wicks on both sides (doji or spinning tops) indicates a trend change.

- The bearish candles with no higher wick indicate a strong downtrend.

Kagi Charts

Kagi charts are very similar to point-and-figure charts, but the X and O columns are replaced by simple lines, or sometimes by 'yin' and 'yang' lines.

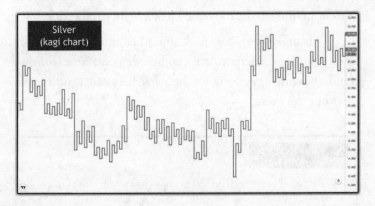

Image 4.9 – A Kagi chart (Silver)

Investors use these charts because they take out the equation of 'time'. The charts only change direction when the security moves by some specific points. They are used to identify long-term reversals.

Conclusion

Doctors use a stethoscope to measure blood pressure and listen to the sounds of the heart, lungs, or intestines. A good doctor can extract valuable information even using an ordinary stethoscope, but even the most advanced stethoscope would not help a lousy doctor.

Similarly, different charts present the information of price fluctuations in different ways. So, a trader should pick any chart they like and should be able to understand the information that it displays. This can help them identify profitable price patterns/opportunities in the stock market and make better trading decisions.

5

Avoid These Stocks to Protect Your Wealth

Whenever a stock market rallies to record highs or all-time highs, it indicates the strength of markets. However, it also creates the perfect breeding ground for stock market fraud.

When it happens, most people feel as if they have missed a fantastic opportunity to make money, and so they become eager to deploy their capital in some stocks. They come to know about a stock that yielded three-digit returns in the last few weeks and they deploy some capital, hoping it will bring them profits.

To their horror, it starts collapsing every day, and within a few days, it reaches single digits. They feel helpless, and they turn into long-term investors in the company and hope it will rise in the future.

Almost all traders and investors have gone through this horrible experience. It is always better to avoid these stocks in order to survive in the stock market.

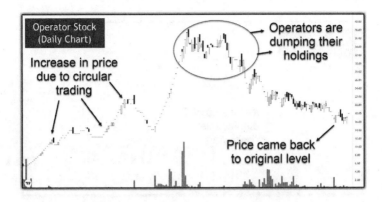

Image 5.1 – The propaganda of an operator stock

Image 5.1 shows how operators work. Initially, they lift the price of a small company through circular trading. Circular trading means a group of people buy and sell the stocks with a mutual agreement until they reach a predefined price level.

These operators chose a small company so that they can quickly lift the price with the help of their group (as small capital is enough for small companies).

When the stock reaches a predefined target, they generate a lot buzz with the help of social media, and once the retail people start buying, they will dump all their holdings and look for other stocks to manipulate.

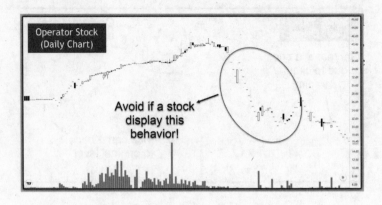

Image 5.2 – Operator stock (Example 1)

Image 5.2 shows an example of an operator stock. Whenever you see a small horizontal line instead of a candle, it indicates that the open, close, high, and low levels are the same, or that trading is not allowed on that day. So it is always better to avoid such stocks.

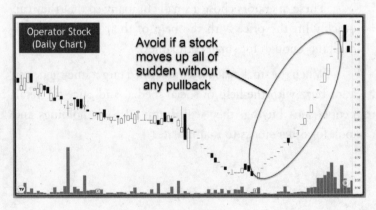

Image 5.3 – Operator stock (Example 2)

Image 5.3 shows another example of an operator stock. In this case, the operators have pushed the price up rapidly. Always remember that a healthy uptrend gives minor pullback before going up. But in the above case, the price has gone up without showing any pullback. Hence, it is always better to avoid such stocks.

6

Different Types of Trading

There are different types of trading in the stock market. You can choose a style that fits your personality and your goals.

For example, if you have a lot of money and want to make money gradually over time, then long-term investments are good for you. If you want to make a lot of money quickly, then short-term trading is better.

Every style has its own advantages and disadvantages. So, it's essential to know about them before you choose one. After all, this is real money we're talking about.

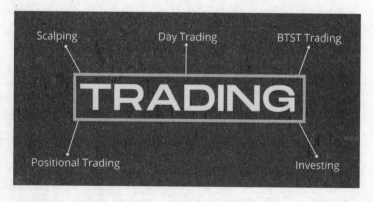

Image 6.1 – Different styles of trading

Here are some different trading styles, based on the holding period of the trade:

- Scalping
- Intraday trading
- BTST trading
- Positional trading or swing trading
- Long-term trading or investment

Scalping

Scalping is a trading method where you trade quickly to make smaller profits from a large number of trades instead of making a large amount of money from one or two trades.

The holding period for scalping is shorter than intraday trading – between 1 minute to 1 hour long.

Scalping got its name because traders who use this style—known as 'scalpers'—enter and exit the market quickly to make small profits from numerous trades throughout the day.

Beginners and intermediate-level traders should avoid scalping as it comes with more risks, and trade execution costs are always high.

Intraday Trading

Intraday trading is also recognized as day trading, and in this type, traders buy and sell the stock on the same day. Here, traders hold their trade from a few minutes to a few hours based on the movement. However, intraday traders don't carry their position overnight and close all their positions before the market closes.

Intraday trading is for people who are active and can make quick decisions. This kind of trading provides more opportunities, but it also comes with more noise. Because of this, it demands quick decision-making and reasonable emotional control. For this reason, beginners should stay away from intraday trading.

BTST Trading (Buy Today and Sell Tomorrow)

In this system, traders buy a stock on one day with the expectation that the price will go up that day and the next. Then they sell it on the next day, making a profit. Some traders use this method to avoid taking delivery of stocks (due to T+n settlement cycles) and also to take advantage of price movements.

STBT trading (sell today and buy tomorrow) is similar to BTST, but it works in the opposite way. In this case, the trader sells first, carries his short position to the next day, and squares it off by buying.

Positional Trading or Swing Trading

Positional trading is a type of trading where you hold your position in the market for an extended period of time. This could be a day, a week, or even a month.

Compared to intraday trading, positional trading allows you to stay in the market for a longer period and make more money in each trade (if your idea was correct).

Traders who do positional trading do not look forward to capturing short-term price movements. Instead, they try to find trends that will last longer and make money from them.

Positional trading is very similar to investing, but there is a crucial difference. People who do positional trading can take both long and short trades, while people who invest can only go long.

Investment

In this method, people aim to buy the shares of fundamentally strong companies and hold them for a few months to a few years. Most people use fundamental analysis to pick stocks to invest in. In some cases, people also use Dow Theory concepts.

> *"The stock market is a device for transferring money from the impatient to the patient."* – Warren Buffett

Conclusion

The internet has helped the stock market and other types of trading to become more popular. The internet has also made it easier for people who aren't experts to trade securities. Trading is more like an art than a science. People can learn about trading by indulging in different types of trading.

Please note that opportunities exist across all timeframes. Hence, it is always essential to pick the trading style that complements your personality. Then you'll have fewer emotions to deal with! So, study all the trading types and understand how they work.

7

Support and Resistance Matter a Lot in Trading

Support and resistance levels are significant price levels where people interested in buying or selling a stock meet. Technical analysts see these price levels as necessary in order to understand the psychology of the market and to assess how much demand and supply there is for a particular stock.

When these support or resistance levels are broken, it is assumed that the number of people interested in buying or selling the stock has changed, which might mean that the new support and resistance levels will be established.

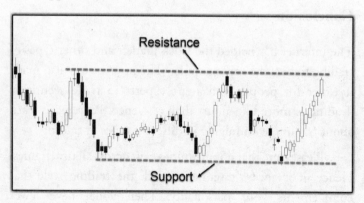

Image 7.1 – Support and resistance levels

Support

The support level is the price at which demand is strong enough to prevent the stock from falling further. In Image 7.1, you can see that it faces difficulty going lower every time the price reaches the support level.

This is because as the price drops and comes near the support level, buyers become more inclined to buy, and sellers become less willing to sell.

Resistance

Resistance is the level at which there are more sellers than buyers. In Image 7.1, you can see that when the price reaches the resistance level, it has a hard time going any higher.

This is because as the price rises and gets closer to the resistance level, sellers become more eager to sell, and buyers become less willing to buy.

Angled Support and Resistance Lines

There is no rule that supports and resistance lines have to be perfectly horizontal lines on the price chart. They can also be slightly angled.

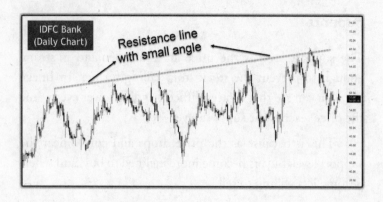

Image 7.2 – A resistance line with a small angle (IDFC)

Image 7.2 shows an example of an angled resistance trend line. Sellers entered the game whenever the price bounced toward the angled resistance line, and their selling pressure pushed the price to the downside.

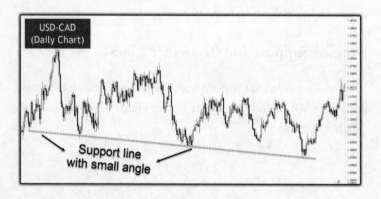

Image 7.3 – A support line with a small angle (USD-CAD)

Image 7.3 shows an example of an angled support line. Whenever the price corrected toward the angled support trend line, buyers entered with some buying, and their force pushed the price toward the upside.

The Psychology Behind Support and Resistance

There are many people involved in the buying and selling of any stock at any given time.

First, let's say there were some buyers of a stock near the support area, which is about 100. They bought the stock when it was trading at 100, and then sold it when it reached 110. This associates a pleasant memory of that particular stock with a price level of 100, and whenever it comes back to 100, they are eager to repurchase it.

The second category of people are observers. They were watching when the price started trading from 100. Now it traded above and came back to 100. These people participate as buyers at the level of 100, hoping it will rise again.

The third category are those investors who aim to accumulate good stocks at a lesser price. They bought the shares at 100, and after it reaches 110, they are sure that it will give a further good move in the future. Hence, they are keen to buy more shares if the price comes back to 100.

There are many more possible scenarios when it comes to trading stocks. If you have traded before, you have probably been through all of these scenarios and know how you feel about each one. You are not alone. Countless people think of the same things as you do, which helps in determining the market psychology behind support and resistance.

Role Reversal of Support and Resistance

An exciting concept about supports and resistances is that their roles are reversed whenever either one is broken. For example, if the price shows a decisive break of the support level, then this support level acts as resistance in the future. Similarly, if the price breaks the resistance level, then the same level acts as support in the future.

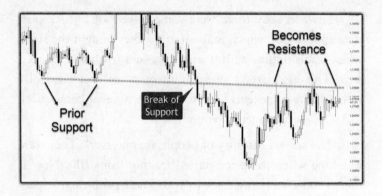

Image 7.4 – The support line acted as resistance

Image 7.4 shows an example in which the prior support level acted as a resistance line. The price breaks the support line in the middle, and later, the same line acts as resistance whenever the price jumps toward that level.

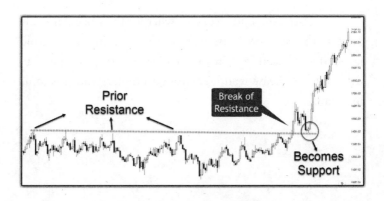

Image 7.5 – The resistance line acted as support

Image 7.5 shows an example in which the prior resistance level acted as a support line. The price breaks the strong resistance line, and later, the same line acts as a support when the price displayed a pullback toward the same level.

Conclusion

Technical analysis (TA) is a simple approach to determine the future price, and support/resistance are simple concepts within TA, which are developed based on human emotions.

Identifying the proper support and resistance trend lines is essential. Drawing trend lines is also an art, and one should learn it through practice. My suggestion is to draw trend lines for 100 charts and get feedback from an expert trader. This simple exercise is guaranteed to improve your skill of drawing trend lines.

Similarly, the knowledge of whether the price has really broken the support/resistance is very important to avoid failed trades. Section 2 in this book is entirely dedicated to this topic, so please read it carefully to understand this topic in detail.

8

Chart Patterns

Stock chart patterns are an essential aspect of technical analysis. They can help you predict when a stock is going to break out or reverse from a critical price level. If you learn to recognize these chart patterns, you can take more profitable trades in the stock market.

Stock chart patterns are a way to analyze how the price of a stock changes over time. You can look at this information for any time period – monthly, weekly, daily, or even intraday.

One of the great things about chart patterns is that they tend to happen again and again. This is something that appeals to our psychology. If you can recognize these patterns early on, you will have a real advantage in the market.

Below are some of the important chart patterns that occur in all the timeframes.

Head and Shoulder

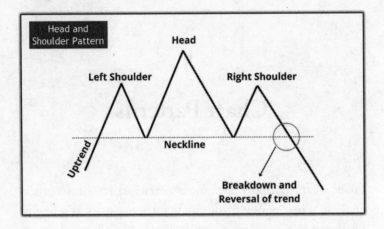

Image 8.1 – The head and shoulders pattern

Head and shoulders is a **bearish chart pattern**. It has a large peak at the center (head) and two minor peaks (shoulders) on either side.

Once the third peak breaks the neckline, it confirms that the prior uptrend is over and the downtrend has started.

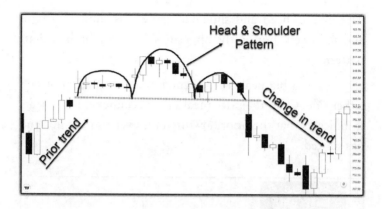

Image 8.2 – The head and shoulders pattern (Example)

Image 8.2 shows an example of a head and shoulders pattern. Many traders target the height of the head (from the neckline) on the downside.

Inverse Head and Shoulders

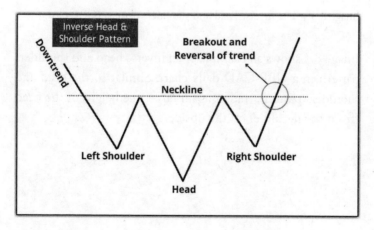

Image 8.3 – The inverse head and shoulders pattern

The inverse head and shoulders pattern is similar to head and shoulders, but on the opposite side. It is a **bullish chart pattern.**

It has a big peak at the center and two small peaks on either side. Once the price breaks the neckline on the upside, it indicates that the prior downtrend is over and the uptrend has started.

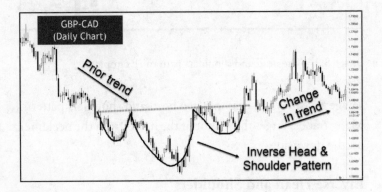

Image 8.4 – The inverse head and shoulders pattern (GBP-CAD)

Image 8.4 shows an example of an inverse head and shoulders pattern in a GBP-CAD daily chart. Similar to the head and shoulders pattern, traders again target the height of the head (from the neckline) on the upside.

Cup and Handle Pattern

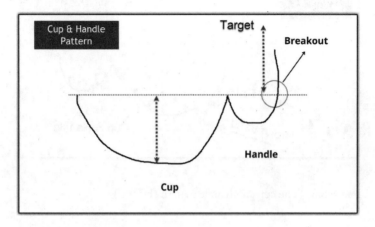

Image 8.5 – The cup and handle pattern

The cup and handle is a **bullish continuation pattern.** Usually, this pattern appears in stocks during a strong uptrend. The cup looks identical to the rounding bottom pattern, indicating the buildup.

After the formation of the cup, it gives a minor retracement (small pullback), which is nothing but a handle.

The break of the handle indicates that all the selling is negated, and the price is ready to give a good upside move.

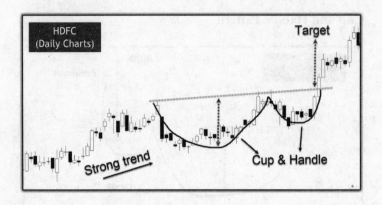

Image 8.6 – The cup and handle pattern (HDFC)

Image 8.6 shows an example of a cup and handle pattern in an HDFC chart. Traders target the height of the cup (from the neckline) on the upside.

Bull Flag Pattern

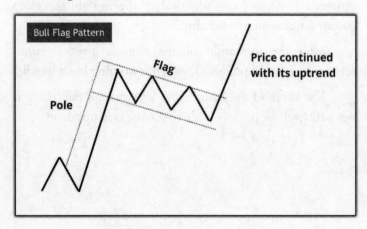

Image 8.7 – The bull flag pattern

The bull flag is also a **bullish continuation pattern.** Typically, it appears in stocks which are in a strong uptrend. It forms a 'pole' first, which indicates a swift rally on the upside.

After the formation of a pole, it gives a small retracement that looks like a flag (as shown in Image 8.7).

The break of the flag indicates that all the selling has been negated, and the price is ready to give a good move on the upside.

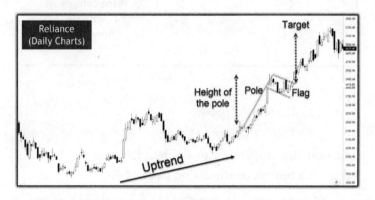

Image 8.8 – The bull flag pattern (Reliance)

Image 8.8 shows an example of a bull flag pattern in a Reliance chart. Traders keep the height of the pole as their target on the upside.

Bear Flag Pattern

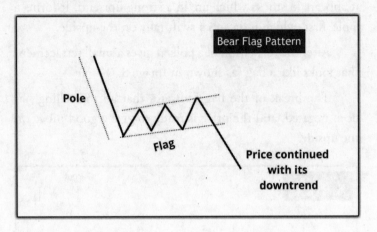

Image 8.9 – The bear flag pattern

The bear flag is identical to the bull flag, but on the other side. It is a **bearish continuation pattern.**

In most cases, it appears in stocks during a strong downtrend. It forms a 'pole' first, which indicates a good fall on the downside.

After the formation of the pole, it gives a slight bounce that looks like a flag. The break of the flag indicates that all the buying has been negated, and the price is ready to give a good move on the downside.

Image 8.10 – The bear flag pattern (Mahanagar Gas)

Image 8.10 shows an example of a bear flag pattern in Mahanagar Gas stock. Once again, traders keep the height of the pole as their target on the downside.

Triangle Pattern (symmetrical, ascending, and descending)

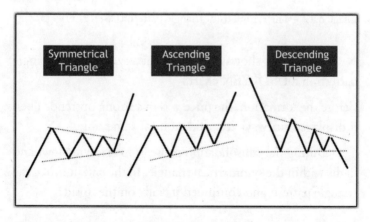

Image 8.11 – The triangle pattern (symmetrical, ascending, and descending)

A triangle pattern is a **consolidation pattern** in between the trends and indicates the continuation of the current trend.

There are three types in the triangle pattern:

1. Symmetrical triangle

2. Ascending triangle

3. Descending triangle

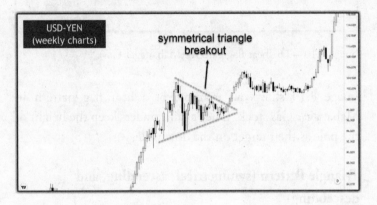

Image 8.12 – The symmetrical triangle pattern (USD-YEN)

Image 8.12 shows an example of a symmetrical triangle pattern in a USD- YEN chart.

Before the formation, the price was in a strong uptrend. Then it displayed sideways consolidation for some time.

During the consolidation phase, it made swing lows and highs within the symmetrical triangle. In the end, it broke the triangle pattern and continued its rally on the upside.

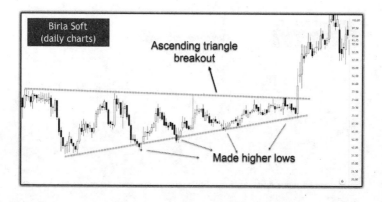

Image 8.13 – The ascending triangle pattern (Birlasoft)

Image 8.13 shows an example of an ascending triangle pattern in Birlasoft stock.

Before the formation, the price displayed sideways consolidation for some time.

During the consolidation phase, it made swing lows and highs within the triangle. It is interesting to note that it made all the highs at the same level, but all lows at a higher level. This is a typical characteristic of ascending triangle.

In the end, it broke the triangle pattern and rallied on the upside. Usually, traders take the triangle's width and target the same level as their target after the breakout.

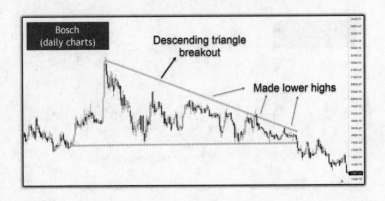

Image 8.14 – The descending triangle pattern (Bosch)

Image 8.14 shows an example of a descending triangle pattern in Bosch stock.

Before the formation, the price displayed sideways consolidation for some time.

During the consolidation phase, it made swing lows and swing highs within the triangle. Again, it is interesting to note that it made all the swing lows at almost the same level, but all swing highs at a lower level. This is a typical characteristic of a descending triangle.

In the end, it broke the triangle pattern and started to fall. Usually, traders take the width of the triangle and target the same level as their target after the breakdown.

Conclusion

Chart patterns are essential tools to help us understand why the price of a stock behaved in a certain way. These patterns show where the market is likely to support or resist a price change, which can help traders decide if they should open a long or short position.

All the chart patterns explained in this chapter are useful technical concepts that help traders to identify the best entry and exit points. However, there is no need to study and remember all of them.

"All you need is one pattern for living."
– Linda Raschke

The above quote from the world-famous trader Linda Raschke conveys a vital message. You can pick any pattern that makes sense to your mind and backtest the same pattern with historical data.

Please note that none of the patterns give 100% accurate results, as the market is dynamic. Hence, it is always good to follow money management rules and risk only a small portion of your capital per trade.

9

Technical Indicators

People who are experts in any field have a toolbox. This could mean different things for different people. For some people, like carpenters and mechanics, their toolboxes are literal. For other people, like lawyers and marketers, their toolboxes are more symbolic, but still just as important.

Experts may not require any technical indicators as they can trade with pure price action, but these technical indicators offer immense help for beginners and intermediate-level traders and algorithmic traders.

There are thousands of technical indicators in technical analysis. All technical indicators available in the stock market are derived from different calculations using the same price information: open, close, high, low, and volume.

Here are some of the most popular and frequently-used indicators in the trading community.

Moving Average (MA)

Moving averages calculate the mean value of price variations over a selected period; thus, they negate all the short-term hikes or quick moves.

The moving average is a lagging indicator, as MAs are calculated using the past price action. As a lagging indicator, MAs are the best tool to confirm a stock trend rather than to predict future direction or momentum.

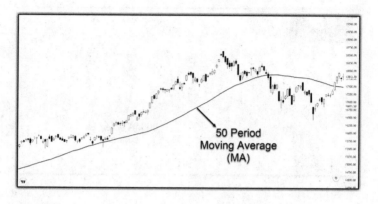

Image 9.1 – A moving average

There are different variations of moving averages. Here are the important types:

Simple moving averages (SMA) takes the candles' closing price for the selected period, calculates the average over the mentioned period, and plots the line on the chart.

Exponential moving averages (EMA) gives more weightage to recent candles, calculates the average of the mentioned period, and plots the line on the chart.

There is not much of a difference between SMA and EMA. SMA is helpful for long-term traders; in contrast, EMA is beneficial for short-term traders.

Moving averages also act as support and resistance. A 50-day or 100-day MA acts as a support when the stock is in an uptrend. Similarly, when the stock is in a downtrend, the same MA acts as a resistance.

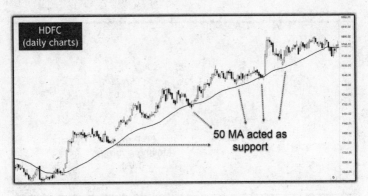

Image 9.2 – A 50 MA acting as support (HDFC)

Image 9.2 is a daily chart of HDFC stock. In this stock, for the selected period, 50 MA acted as support whenever the price gave a pullback.

MA Crossovers

Traders use MA crossovers as their trading strategies. There are many variations of MA crossovers. The simple crossover is when the price crosses a specific MA, which indicates a potential change in the trend.

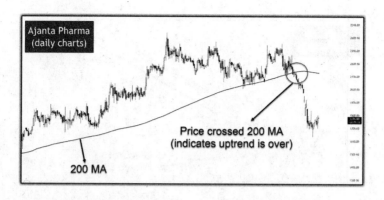

Image 9.3 – 200 MA crossover (Ajanta Pharma)

Image 9.3 shows a daily chart of Ajanta Pharma, and 200 MA is applied on the same chart. In the end, the price crossed 200 MA below, which indicates the end of the uptrend and the beginning of a downtrend.

Another strategy is to use two moving averages – shorter- and longer-moving averages (50-200, 10-50, 15-200, etc.).

For example, we take 5 MA as the shorter MA and 50 MA as the longer MA. Whenever the **short**-term MA crosses above the long-term MA, it is a buy signal (also called a **golden** cross), and whenever the short-term MA crosses below the long-term MA, it is a sell signal (also called a death cross).

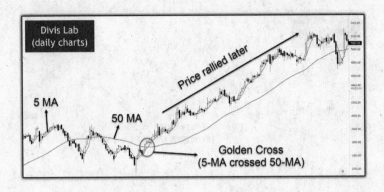

Image 9.4 – A golden crossover (Divis Lab)

Image 9.4 shows an example of a golden crossover in Divis Lab stock. 5 MA crossed 50 MA from the downside, and later, the price rallied on the upside.

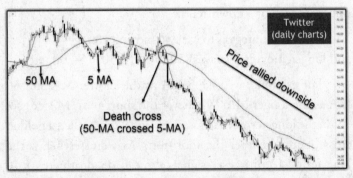

Image 9.5 – A death crossover (Twitter)

Image 9.5 shows an example of death crossover in Twitter stock. 5 MA crossed 50 MA from the upside, and later, the price rallied on the downside.

MACD Indicator

MACD acts as both a momentum oscillator and a trend follower. Technically, it belongs to the momentum oscillator category; however, it is not common to use it to identify overbought and oversold situations like any other oscillator. It is used to determine the trend or any change in the trend.

The MACD fluctuates above and below the zero line, based on whether the two MAs converge or diverge.

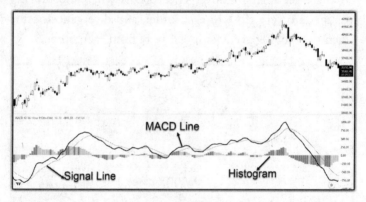

Image 9.6 – The MACD indicator

The MACD indicator consists of three components:

1. MACD line

2. Signal line

3. MACD Histogram

The MACD line is drawn after subtracting 26 days EMA from 12 days EMA (MACD line = 12 EMA – 26 EMA).

A **signal line** is a simple 9 days EMA.

The **MACD histogram** is plotted using the difference between the MACD line and the signal line. It will have a positive value when the MACD line crosses above the signal line, and it will show a negative value when the MACD line crosses below the signal line.

As the name suggests, MACD is all about the **convergence** and **divergence** of the two moving averages on the price chart. Convergence occurs when the moving averages are very close to each other, and divergence occurs when the moving averages move away from each other.

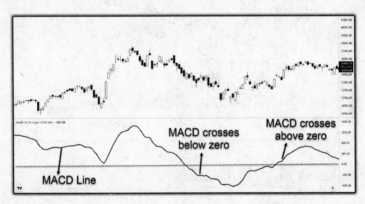

Image 9.7 – Trading based on the MACD line with zero

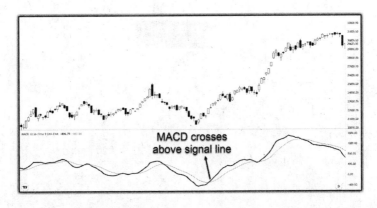

Image 9.8 – Trading based on the MACD line and signal line

Many traders use MACD in different ways. However, below are the two popular methods of using MACD:

1. When the MACD line crosses above zero, it is considered bullish, and it is viewed as bearish when the MACD crosses below zero.

2. When the MACD line crosses above the signal line, it is considered bullish. Similarly, when the MACD crosses below, the signal line is bearish.

Images 9.7 and 9.8 show examples for both methods.

Bollinger Bands

John Bollinger developed the Bollinger Bands indicator in the mid-1980s. It consists of three different lines:

1. A 20-period SMA as the midline

2. Two lines as two standard deviations above and below the midline

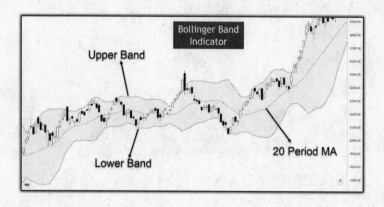

Image 9.9 – A Bollinger Band indicator

The distance between the upper and lower bands is based on the standard deviation. Hence, they contrast and expand based on the price variations, which is nothing but volatility.

If the volatility is high, the bands will expand automatically, and if the volatility is less, the bands will contract. Hence, these Bollinger Bands can also identify the overbought and oversold conditions in any stock.

When these bands squeeze due to low volatility, there is a high probability of a sharp and quick price bounce in any direction. It is recognized as the Bollinger Band Squeeze trading method. Some traders use this method. As the price moves in any one direction, the bands will slowly expand.

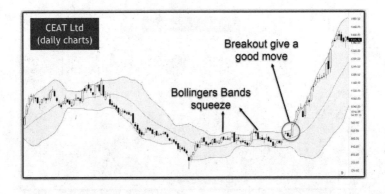

Image 9.10 – A Bollinger Band squeeze breakout (Ceat Ltd)

Image 9.10 shows an example of the Bollinger Band squeeze breakout trading method. The price kept on hugging the upper band in an uptrend. Hence, it makes sense to carry the trade until it is attached with the upper band (or we can also trail stop-loss). However, in the case of a sideways move, the price will oscillate between the upper and lower bands.

Stochastic Indicator

A stochastic indicator is an oscillator indicator that compares the closing price to the range of its prices over a given (or selected) period in the selected stock. Then it plots the values within the range of 0 to 100.

A reading of 80 and above indicates it is overbought, and a reading of 20 and below indicates it is oversold.

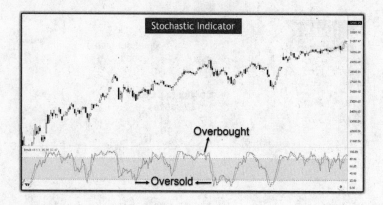

Image 9.11 – A stochastic indicator

We should not look for a long trade just because stochastics reached the oversold region. It is necessary to use some confirmation (like a candlestick pattern or chart pattern) before taking a trade, because the price can stay in the oversold or overbought zone for longer periods in a trending environment.

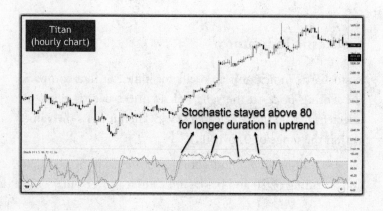

Image 9.12 – A stochastic indicator in an uptrend (Titan)

In Image 9.12, the stochastic indicator stayed above 80 for an extended period in an uptrend. Hence, we should plan a trade only when the price is coming out of that range. For example, you can plan a long trade if the price takes support at the support line and the stochastics move above 20 (from the downside).

Similarly, we can plan a short trade when the price takes resistance at the resistance trend line and the stochastics move below 80 (from the upside).

ADX Indicator

The ADX indicator is a popular indicator used to identify the strength of the trend of a stock. It has three components: the ADX line, +DMI, and –DMI.

An ADX line above **25 is considered a strong trend** (either an uptrend or a downtrend). In addition to that:

- if the +DMI line is above –DMI, then it is considered that the bulls are in control

- if –DMI is above +DMI, the bears are in control over the bulls.

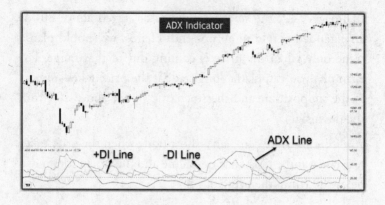

Image 9.13 – The ADX indicator

Traders can plan a long trade only if the ADX line is above 25 and +DI is above -DI, if the price takes support at the trend line, or if the price breaks the resistance line.

Similarly, we can plan a short trade if the ADX line is above 25 and if –DMI is above +DMI and if the price takes resistance at the trend line, or if the price breaks the support line.

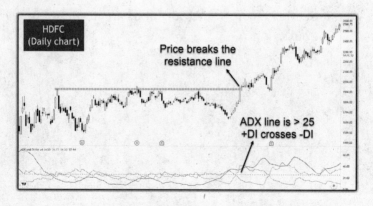

Image 9.14 – A long trade idea using the ADX indicator (HDFC)

Image 9.14 shows an example of a long trade idea using the ADX indicator in an HDFC daily chart. The price breaks the resistance line, and at the same time, +DI crosses above the –DI line, and the ADX line is already above 25.

Hence, it is better to plan a long trade in this case.

RSI Indicator

J. Welles Wilder developed the RSI indicator, and it was first introduced in his book New Concepts in Technical Systems in 1978.

The basic formula for RSI is:

RSI = 100 – [100 / (1 + (Average gain / Average loss))]

The average gain or loss used in this formula is the average percentage gain or loss during a look-back period.

RSI uses 14 days as the standard period to calculate its value. However, we can change these settings.

The RSI indicator oscillates between 0 and 100. Traditionally, traders consider that the stock is in an overbought situation when the RSI is above 70 and oversold when the RSI is below 30.

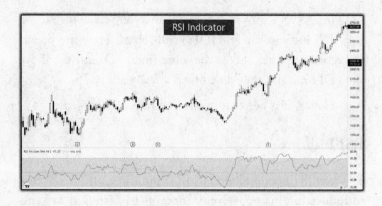

Image 9.15 – The RSI indicator

However, similar to the stochastic indicator, the RSI indicator can also stay above 70 in an uptrend and below 30 in a downtrend.

A better use of RSI is mentioned below:
RSI is above 60 – Uptrend RSI is below 40 – Downtrend
RSI is between 40 to 60 – Sideways trend

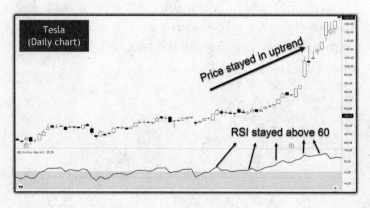

Image 9.16 – The RSI indicator in an uptrend (Tesla)

Image 9.16 gives an example of RSI behavior in an uptrend in Tesla stock. It stayed above 60 levels in the complete uptrend.

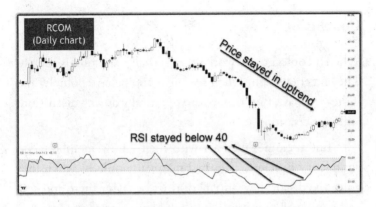

Image 9.17 – The RSI indicator in a downtrend (RCOM)

Image 9.17 gives an example of RSI behavior in a downtrend in RCOM stock. It stayed below 40 levels when the price remained in a downtrend.

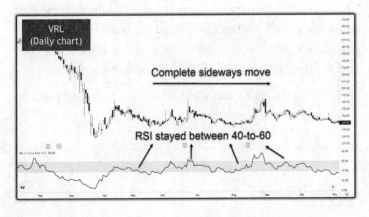

Image 9.18 – RSI Indicator in Sideways Trend (VRL)

Image 9.18 gives an example of RSI behavior in a sideways trend in VRL stock. It stayed between 40 to 60 levels when the price stayed in a sideways trend.

Conclusion

When people go to work, they usually act professionally. They greet everyone when see them and behave politely, and if they're smart, they behave diplomatically during discussions and conversations.

But at home, they act with their family members in a completely different, informal manner. Similarly, when they go to the disco, they display distinct behavior there and sing and dance to the music. And they'd have a great time, too!

Similarly, all the technical indicators behave differently in different market conditions. In an uptrend, they behave in a certain way. In a downtrend, they behave differently. And in a sideways market, again, they act differently.

Hence, it doesn't make sense to apply multiple indicators to the chart and study them. Smart traders look at how one particular indicator behaves in different market conditions and use that information while making trading decisions.

Do you want to use multiple indicators, or do you aim to become a smart trader?

10

How Successful Traders Develop a Trading System

Let us imagine a hypothetical scenario. You know how to drive a regular car, and one day your friend gives you the keys to a Formula One racecar and forces you to participate in an official Formula One race.

Can you imagine the outcome of this situation? It's damn scary, isn't it?

Trading in the stock market is quite similar. Millions of people participate in it every day, and many experts dedicate their entire lives to this game.

When you take a trade, you are fighting against them. If you are not well prepared, they will crush you in minutes.

To achieve success in trading, you should be clear about two aspects:

1. What kinds of trades to **participate in**

2. What types of trades to **avoid**

Unfortunately, most people only focus on the first point and ignore the second one. If you observe carefully, most traders take trades whenever the market gives a good move, but only experts avoid trades when the market is not showing any opportunities.

Most people only focus on taking trades, and hence they ignore mastering the second point (avoiding trades). The only way to attain mastery in both aspects is by following a proper plan, which is nothing but a trading system.

A trading system is a set of rules that a trader uses to make decisions while trading stocks (or any trading instruments).

A trading system outlines what types of trades a trader can take, which markets they are allowed to trade in, what kind of setups the trades may be based on, how much risk they are willing to take on when they are allowed to trade, and how to manage their trades (entry, exit, and stop-loss).

How can Backtesting Ease Your Pain?

Some people argue that backtesting is not necessary and is a waste of time. Their logic is that live market conditions are always different when compared to historical data.

But I can't entirely agree with their logic. Let me explain in detail.

Cricket is one of the most famous sports on this planet after football. It is pretty similar to baseball. **The only significant difference is that a batsman has to hit the ball only after pitchin**g. In baseball, the ball is thrown directly toward the batsman, but in cricket, bowlers will pitch the ball before it reaches the batsman.

Because of this one change, many factors come into the picture – soil quality, grass on the pitch, wind speed, etc. The reason is simple – all these factors contribute to the **ball's bounce or turn** before it reaches the batsman.

Hence, each country's playing conditions are different. For example, the Indian subcontinent (India, Sri Lanka, Pakistan, and Bangladesh) pitches offer immense help to spinners and allow batters to score more runs easily, whereas pitches in New Zealand and England immensely help fast bowlers, but batters face a tough time scoring runs in such conditions.

What happens if the Indian cricket team travels to England and starts playing World Cup matches directly?

Indian batters are more likely to struggle (at least in the first few matches), and there is a high possibility of failure. Do you agree?

Do you think their performance would be better if the cricketers traveled to England a few weeks in advance, did some net practice for a few days, and played friendly matches with local teams?

Definitely! They would get accustomed to the variance of bounce conditions.

The same logic goes for backtesting.

It prepares traders for facing dynamic market conditions by giving them the necessary conviction in a trading system. It does so by showing them the results of the system when using historical data.

The advantages of backtesting are:

- It indicates whether there is an edge in your trading system without risking your hard-earned money

- If your trading strategy is profitable in backtesting, then it gives you the confidence to stick to it in live trading.

How to Perform Backtesting

To perform backtesting on a trading strategy, we need clarity on the following aspects:

1) What are the conditions for ENTRY?

2) Where is the initial STOP-LOSS?

3) What is the trading TIMEFRAME?

4) What is the EXIT criteria?

5) How much MONEY DO YOU RISK per trade?

6) How many trades do you take IN A DAY?

There are two ways of backtesting a trading strategy – either manually or by coding.

In the manual method, a trader will manually check the entry/stop-loss/exit conditions by looking at the chart and logging the results in a spreadsheet. In the end, they will calculate the overall P&L of the system.

In the coding method, a trader defines his trading strategy by coding it (using Java, Python, or Amibroker), runs it against historical data, and gets the P&L details of the system.

For better understanding, here is a simple trading system with all the rules.

MA Intraday System (Only Long Trades)

<u>Timeframe</u> – 30 minutes.

<u>Entry Rule</u> – Whenever 5 MA crosses above 50 MA.

<u>Stop-Loss</u> – 0.5% from the entry price. For example, if the entry was made at 10000, then stop-loss is at 9950.

<u>Exit Rule</u> – Either stop-loss hits or 5 MA crosses below 50 MA.

<u>Risk Management</u> – Risk only 2% of your capital per trade. If the capital is 2,00,000, then risk only 4,000 per trade.

<u>How Many Trades in a Day</u> – Only 2 trades.

Please note that the above rules are just an example to give you some clarity on all the necessary factors required for backtesting. Once traders shortlist all these rules for their trading ideas, they can proceed with backtesting. I suggest backtesting a trading idea with a minimum of 10 years of historical data.

Example of a Trading System Along With Backtesting Results

Please note that the idea of sharing a trading system and backtesting results is to encourage traders to develop their own trading system, not to use it as it is.

Also note that the utmost caution has been taken while backtesting this trading strategy. However, there is still the possibility of a minor deviation if there are any discrepancies in the data or the code.

82-MA Intraday System

Timeframe – 15-minute chart

Backtested Instrument – Banknifty

Entry Rule –

Long Trade

Price should cross and close above 82 MA + the next candle should break the high of the crossover candle (entry comes at the high of the crossover candle)

Short Trade

Price should cross and close below 82 MA + the next candle should break the low of the crossover candle (entry comes at the low of the crossover candle)

Stop-Loss – 0.5% from the entry price.

Exit Rule – Either stop-loss hits or EOD closes (market closes).

Risk Management – Only 2 lots for ₹3,50,000 capital.

How Many Trades in a Day – Only 2 trades.

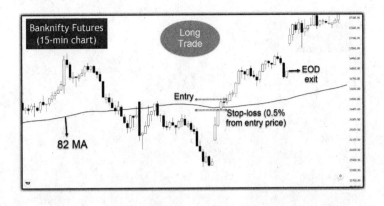

Image 10.1 – A long trade (Example)

Image 10.1 shows an example of a long trade. Entry comes when the price crosses and closes above 82-MA (from the downside), and the next candle breaks the high of the crossover candle.

Entry – 36499

Stop-loss – 36316

Exit – EOD exit, as the price did not hit stop-loss.

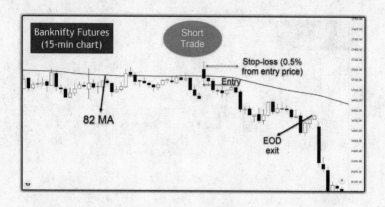

Image 10.2 – A short trade (Example)

Image 10.2 shows an example of a short trade. Entry comes when the price crosses and closes below 82-MA (from the upside), and the next candle breaks the low of the crossover candle.

Entry – 37051

Stop-loss – 37236

Exit – EOD exit, as the price did not hit stop-loss.

Backtesting Settings

Initial Capital – ₹3,50,000

Trading Instrument – Banknifty Futures

Timeframe – 15-minute charts

Trading Window – 2010 to 2020

Position Sizing – Fixed 2 Lots (No increment with capital)

Transaction/Slippage Cost – 0.002%

EOD exit – 3.15 p.m. (IST – Indian Standard Time)

Backtesting Results

Initial Capital – ₹3,50,000

Ending Capital – ₹14,34,289 (14 lakh+)

(PS: This capital will increase multiple times if I increase the position size along with an increase in the capital, but my aim is to show you how to backtest a trading system, not to trigger your emotions.)

Accuracy – 41%

Profit Factor – 1.4

Maximum Drawdown – 15% of the capital

Consecutive Losing Trades – 10 trades in one stretch

Total Number of Trades – 1,352 in 10 years

In this manner, one should shortlist the rules of their trading system and backtest it with historical data before taking trades in the live market.

Final Words

I genuinely hope that you have gained some useful knowledge on breakout trading from this book. This concept helped me immensely in my trading career, and I hope it will also play a decisive role in your life. I hope to spread this positive impact to the lives of others through this book.

Now that you have read my book, I ask that you please do one of two things (or both) if you have some time.

1. If you enjoyed this book, PLEASE leave a kind review on Amazon. As an independent author, word of mouth is my only advertising. Amazon link: - **https://amz. run/3SPi**

2. No book is perfect. If there are any errors or omissions, or if there is anything you would like to see added, please email me at indrazith.s@gmail.com. I promise a quick, personal response.

I would LOVE to hear your success stories, comments, and suggestions! Signing off.

Indrazith Shantharaj

Twitter - @indraziths

Other titles by Indrazith Shantharaj,
published by Manjul Publishing House

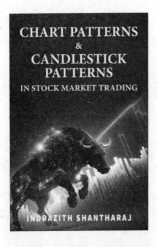

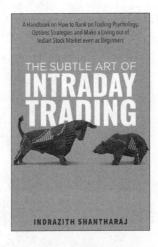

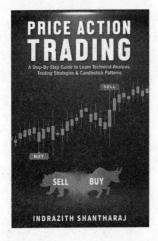

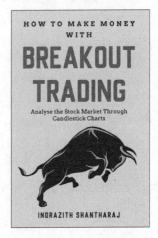